ALEX ROLLINS

40 days Tour Of Northern Iceland

Ultimate Travel Guide

Contents

Introduction

It's a holiday. That's one of the fantastic moments that everyone is waiting for, and whenever it's the holidays, what usually comes to most people's minds is VACATION. Yes, right. You are leaving your home, traveling to a new destination, seeing new places, and meeting new people. So this time, you want to travel to the Northern part of Iceland. That's a fantastic decision because you are about to go to one of the best places you will ever find in the world.

Iceland is filled with nature; you will find multiple unique hot springs, possibly hike through a glacier there, and have fantastic memories that will last you a lifetime. In fact, you will have enough room for your imagination to run wild; in Northern Iceland, you will find hidden people and tales of trolls that are only found in the fantasy realms.

And amazingly, there are no travel restrictions now, be it the pre-departure tests or vaccination; all were scrapped in 2022. Even wearing mandatory masks in 2020 is now left to your discretion, and if, unfortunately, you experience the COVID-19 symptoms there, you will receive a test free of charge.

In this chapter, we will look at the necessary informa-

tion concerning Northern Iceland, its annual weather condition, culture, and what you need to pack in your suitcase before you start your beautiful trip.

So what are the best areas to have fun in North Iceland? Well, that's why we are here. We took our time to write this specific book containing all the information related to North Iceland, including destinations you can enjoy, such as the Siglufjordur, Grimsey, Laufas Turf Homes, Husavik, and other incredible places. We didn't forget to mention the North Iceland culture, their annual weather, and what you need to pack in your traveling suitcase. So patiently continue reading to have a head start.

History of Northern Iceland and other necessary information

If this is the first time you travel to North Iceland, we thought giving you a little history of the country would help. Iceland is a European country that became an independent republic on 17 June 1944. Its first president after independence was Sveinn Björnsson. Iceland is located on the Nordic island in the North Atlantic ocean.

Iceland is divided into eight regions, the capital region, the Southern peninsula, the west, the west fjords, the Northwest, the Northeast, the South, and the East. We will focus on the Northern region. The capital of North Iceland is **Akureyri,** the fourth-most famous town in Iceland. North Iceland has many historical landmarks, untouched nature, and diverse, vibrant culture.

Annual weather conditions in Northern Iceland

The famous city in North Iceland is Akureyri, so we will use the weather conditions there to describe the climate changes.

●January and February

January is a winter month in North Iceland, so the weather is generally poor. It has the highest cold temperature, up to 2°C (36°F) in the daytime, with an average of 7 hours of sunshine coupled with snow and rainfall. And -4°C (25°F) at night. February is also the same, except it has an average of 36 hours of sunshine.

●March

Some areas experience cold in March. The temperature usually ranges from 1°C (33°F) to 3°C (37°F) in the daytime and -3°C (26°F) at night. It has an average of 77 hours of sunlight coupled with snow and rainfall.

●April

April is sunny and has an average of 125 hours of sunshine with little snow and rainfall. The temperature usually ranges from 3°C (37°F) to 6°C (43°F) during the daytime, and at night, it drops to -1°C (31°F) and -3°C (27°F)

●May

May contains an average of 169 hours of sunshine with slight rainfall. It's a moderate sunny month with temperatures ranging from 6°C (43°F) to 10°C (51°F) during the daytime, and at night, it drops to 3°C (38°F) and 1°C (33°F)

●June

June is also a moderately sunny month, with an average of 189 hours of sunlight. The temperature ranges from 9°C (49°F) cold to 14°C (56°F) in the daytime and 7°C (44°F) to 4°C (39°F) at night.

●July and August

July and August are summer months; they are the warmest months in Iceland. The temperature ranges from 14°C (57°F) during the daytime to 9°C (48°F) at night. The weather in these months can be unpleasant and tolerable depending on your area. July has an average of 154 hours of sunlight, while August has an average of 136 hours of sunshine.

●September

September weather can also be unpleasant and tolerable at the same time, depending on where you are living. The temperature is cold, ranging from 8°C (46°F) to 11°C (52°F) in the daytime, and at night, it drops to 5°C (42°F) and 3°C (37°F). The average sunshine is 85 hours throughout the month.

●October

October weather is generally poor; it's the wettest month in North Iceland, with the temperature ranging from 6°C (43°F) in the daytime and 1°C (34°F) at night. The sunshine lasts an average of 50 hours throughout the month.

●November

November is a cold month with snow and rainfall. It has 15 hours of average sunlight throughout the month, with a temperature of 4°C (38°F) in the daytime and -2°C (28°F) at night.

●December

Like January, December is also a winter month in North Iceland. The cold temperature in the daytime is around 3°C (37°F), and at night, it drops to about -4°C (26°F).

The magnificent Northern Lights

One of the tremendous and look-forward reasons most people travel to North Iceland is the magnificent Northern Lights, also known as Aurora Borealis, which is among the most spectacular shows in the world. You can see it from August ending to mid-April. The Northern Lights are clearly and crisply displayed in the sky at night; you will see dancing flickering veils of lights in green, red, or white. Curious about what makes the lights? Modern science explains it is caused by electricity. Linked to the sun, tiny particles called electrons, and protons resulting from the solar wind's electric storms are trapped in the Earth's magnetic field, where they start to spiral back and forth following the magnetic force lines surrounding the magnetic pole. So when trying to enter the magnetic trap, some escape and come into the atmosphere on Earth and hit the molecules. The effect leads the molecule to glow and create those lights.

White and green are the primary hues; however, the colors tend to change depending on pressure and composition in the altitude variation. Since the pressure is low at high altitudes, oxygen molecules stuck by tiny solar wind particles produce a reddish glow. And because of the high pressure at low altitudes, particles that collide with nitrogen molecules have a greenish tinge and sometimes reddish at the lower border.

While this is an explanation made by modern science, ancestors believed that this phenomenon was another matter different from what science has described. But as a visitor, forget about the cause and enjoy your visit. Appreciate the beautiful scenery of the Northern Lights, which is impressively spectacular. (Later, we will discuss the destination where you will get the best Northern Lights photography).

The Northern Iceland Culture

As we know, culture is defined as people's way of life. This includes their food, clothes, currency, language, religion, mode of transportation, and much more. We will look at each of the Northern Iceland cultures in detail.

●Food

The nature around them inspires the food Northern Icelanders eat. In this part of the world, there are multiple free-roaming sheep, cod, herring, char, and many more. The foods here are mostly pure, with fewer GMOs and artificial ingredients. Most of the foods in North Iceland are seafood, rye bread and butter, fermented shark, lamb, skyr, pylsur, and many other sumptuous meals. You will also find world-known delicacies such as ice cream, cheese, and cake. You might also find restaurants that specifically make other dishes known in other countries, so there is a high chance you will get foods you are familiar with in your country or something similar.

●Language

The national language in North Iceland, or Iceland, is called Icelandic. The language is related to Faroese and Western Norwegian. However, if you understand English, you can perfectly communicate with them because English is the second language in the country, so nearly every citizen there can speak it fluently. Again, many Icelanders speak other languages like Danish, German, Spanish, and French. So if any of these is your language, congratulations, you won't encounter any issues communicating in North Iceland.

●**Religion**

From a survey done in 2020, Iceland consists of 75% of people practicing Christianity, 21% not practicing any religion, 1.3% practicing Ásatrúarfélagio, and 2.1% practicing other religions.

●**Clothes**

Although most Icelanders wear casual clothes, you might see the locals wearing knitted wool sweaters no matter the season. This is their traditional outfit called lopapeysa.

●**Health Care**

The North Iceland healthcare system operates eighteen health clinics, four hospitals, and three nursing homes. It offers medical and nursing assistance, including general nursing care, infant and maternity service, vaccinations, and many more.

●**Mode of transportation**

The mode of transportation in Northern Iceland is by car. Trains aren't available in North Iceland, so they only have options for buses, flights, taxis, and private vehicles.

●**Currency**

Iceland's official currency is the **Icelandic Króna (ISK).**

What you should pack in your traveling suitcase

No matter the season, you are traveling to North Iceland. It would be best to pack clothes that will suffice for all climate conditions. So, what you should put in your suitcase should include the following:

●Lightweight woolens or cardigan
●Rainproof coat
●Gloves

●Scarf

●Hat

●Swimsuit

●Towel

●Thermal underwear

●Socks

●Small backpack to put daily necessities and

●Sturdy shoes.

To get a better view of what to pack in your bag when traveling, check above for weather information about your trip month.

Chapter 2

In this chapter, we will look at ten unique places you can visit, including how to reach the place, where to lodge, the dining areas, destinations to have fun, and where to get your best memories.

Places to visit from day 1 to day 10

Day 1: Siglufjordur

Siglufjordur is one of the fantastic North Iceland places worth visiting. Forget about the scenery; even the road to reach there, **road 76,** is among the best scenic routes in Iceland, coupled with the stunning surroundings.

Let's look at a brief history of Siglufjordur.

The area is close to the Arctic circle, less than 40km. The town is a quaint fishing destination and the Northernmost area of the Iceland mainland. The city doesn't only have beautiful nature but also has a fascinating history.

Siglufjordur was a small fishing village that the locals call Sigló. It was fully established in 1915. The fishing industry became more recognized in the city, and it became the world's herring capital. However, the fishing success of the place became its downfall due to stock decline caused by the exploitation of marine resources and overfishing; by 1960, the herring which made the city famous slowly disappeared.

The city was then forced to find a new business, which grew and became a tourist center. In the 20th century, the town was regarded as among the top settlements in Iceland. The transportation link to the place further improved in 2010 after the opening of the Hedinsfjurdur tunnel. Visitors can now visit Sigló from Ring Road or Akureyri daily.

So what can you do in Siglufjordur as a visitor?

Although some of the activities are seasonal, you can do multiple things there. Remember, no matter the time you visit the city, you will find the trip worthwhile. Some of the things you can do in Siglufjordur include:

● **Visit Siglufjordur Marina**

The Siglufjordur Marina is one of the most beautiful towns in North Iceland. It has picture-perfect candy-colored houses, abundant wildflowers, Sigló marina, and a picturesque location in the fjord. Let's not forget about the beautiful **Siglufjordur Marina Village**.

You will find beautiful colorful wooden buildings housing the Hannes Boy Restaurant and Kaffi Raudka that will draw your attention instantly and make you want to stay longer. If you travel to the town in summer, do well to get yourself a drink or meal at the restaurant and find a place to sit on the terrace outside to watch the hustle and bustle of the harbor nearby.

● Siglufjörður Harbor

Siglufjordur contains up to 18 species of bird life nearing 2000 in number. In the Siglufjordur harbor, you will see the actual port working. Dozens of fishermen are returning to shore after catching fish all day. A hundred boats filled with fish crates will return to the town. This site is quite fascinating and an experience you won't forget quickly.

You can walk around the boats, and if you are traveling with children, have fun by making them identify the types of fish in the boat.

● Herring Era Museum

If there is one thing you should make sure you don't miss during your visit to North Iceland, then it should be the Herring Era Museum, which contains the history in its glamour Herring Era days. The museum is designed for both young and old to have fun.

The locals affectionately describe the Herring Era as an adventure era when the city was still a famous town; before the Herring Era period greatly influenced the entire country. The city's success is often compared to the gold rush and referred to as the Atlantic Klondike or the golden age of Siglufjordur.

The importance of the era to Icelanders can never be overestimated. During that period, the whole of Iceland received 20% of its income from the herring. A whole 20% came from the city alone, which was home to more than ten thousand workers. Some of the locals believed the Herring Era was what shaped

Iceland's unique culture. The Herring Era Museum is among the largest seafaring and industry museums, and they usually celebrate the golden age in the museum.

When you visit the Herring Era Museum, you will enjoy it and even feel like history is alive with how it exhibits, demonstrates, and even folk music to assist you in experiencing the town's lively atmosphere when it was in its glory days. In the museum, you can learn more about fishing processes and see ships and boats used in the era.

The museum nicely and carefully preserves a salting station. At times, they organize a show to describe the salting processes.

The museum's opening hours are 1 pm to 5 pm in May and September, 10 am to 6 pm from June to August, and by Appointment from October to April.

● Folk Music Center

The ticket for the Herring Era Museum entry is also attached with access to the Folk Music Center, which is situated in the former home of the Reverend Bjarni Porsteinsson, who was regarded as the **Father of Siglufjordur.** The Folk Music Center is a small musical instrument museum and an excellent opportunity to connect to Icelandic Folk Music. You will hear people's recordings singing Icelandic Folk Music, chanting epic rhymes called *rimur,* and singing Icelandic nursery rhymes. And if you like, you can watch musicians perform while playing the traditional Icelandic zither called *langspil.*

Another Siglufjordur calendar highlight is the five days Folk

Music festivals that happen on the first Wednesday of every July. The festival doesn't only focus on Icelandic and Scandinavian folk music, which they celebrate via dances, concerts, and parties, but also highlights other musical types from all over the world.

The opening hours for the Folk Music Center are from June to August, from 12 pm to 6 pm.

● Segull 67 Brewery

The Segull 67 is a beer brewery center owned by a local family. They are well known, and you can find their beer in most liquor shops in Iceland. However, going to Segull 67 is beyond the beer itself because it links the town's history, fishing history, and three generations of beer producers. You will also find a guided tour there that will assist you in learning more about its origin.

Segull 67 is authentic and exceptional. And aside from beer, you can enjoy musical performances with a live band or poetry some evenings. The name Segull is a unique name derived from the Icelandic language, which means 'magnet.' You will even see it in their logo, a magnet needle on a compass, and the number 67 is the lucky number of the family that owns the store. The grandfather of the current generation of people managing the store drives a truck, F67, and a boat with the number S167.

● Chocolate

Your visit to Siglufjordur would be incomplete if you didn't go to the **Chocolate shop** owned by a local artist, **Frída Gylfadóttir.** In the shop, you can find a lot of handmade artisanal chocolates and fine coffee. (If you're anything like me, coffee and chocolate in the same place are almost synonymous with Heaven's gates. Almost.) You will also see some of her art pieces, mainly dedicated to Icelandic horses. All displayed items in the shop are for sale, including chocolates, which make a nice souvenir, arts, crafts, and paintings.

The Chocolate shop's opening hours are Thursday to Sunday from 1 pm to 6 pm.

● **Hiking**

If you want to enjoy natural beauty, this is a perfect spot. You can go hiking in summer and skiing in winter. You will see many high mountains of Trollaskagi that dominate the town. Siglufjordur is one of the best places to go hiking, as you will see a lot of glaciated mountains, valleys, lakes, and black sandy beaches. You will find hiking maps in the Herring Era Museum that help you identify easy and challenging trails. You can also get the map from the hotel where you lodge or take guided hiking tours. If you visit in June, you can join their hiking week at the end of the month, where the locals will give you a daily guided tour.

And if you visit in summer or late autumn, you may come across berries that grow on the town's hillsides. The most common are the bilberries, which resemble blueberries. You can pick and eat them if they are growing in public areas.

●**Swimming pool**

You will find a very inviting swimming pool in Siglufjordur. The swimming pool is big and attached to a sauna, outdoor hot bath, and gym.

●**Midnight Sun**

Siglufjordur is located high, so get ready to experience the midnight sun, usually from June to July. You will see the sun shining brightly at night and watch it fall to the horizon and rise again. And if you don't want to watch this, carry a sleeping mask in your traveling bag if you are visiting in summer.

●**The Northern Lights**

From Siglufjordur, you can also watch the Northern Lights in winter. Just check the Aurora forecast and go out to chase them. And although it's not the best place to have a perfect view because of the light pollution, you can at least find a dark spot in the areas nearby to watch them. Remember, avoid parking on the road!

●**Skiing**

Skardosdalur is one of the best skiing areas in North Iceland, having four lifts and ten ski slopes. The area is close to Siglufjordur, just a 10-15 minute drive. In addition, you will also find a cross-country ski trail near Hólsdalur. The site is steadily becoming more popular.

What's the best time to visit Siglufjordur?

Although the town is a year-round tourist center, it's best to visit in summer. Summer days are longer, so you can have multiple outdoor activities, access nature, drive or walk on a good road, and all the things in the town are open. And yet, if you can't visit in summer, you can go in winter and enjoy many activities such as skiing and watching the Northern Lights. In winter, you make appointments ahead of time to visit some places like the Herring Era Museum because it's not always open in winter.

●**How to reach Siglufjordur**

If you land at the Akureyri airport, Siglufjordur is about 80 km, a 1h 15 mins drive. Negotiate a single-lane tunnel between Ólafsfjödur and Siglufjordur.

●**Accommodations**

You will find plenty of accommodations there; the cheaper and nicer one is the **Sigló Hotel**. You will be glad to book the hotel after seeing the building and the surroundings. There is also the expensive accommodation, the super luxurious **Deplar Farm** situated close to Siglufjordur. The price of a room here starts at around €2,550 per night for two people, and the minimum stay requirement is two nights. This place is the best if you are the type that loves meeting celebrities and tycoons and your budget is unlimited.

●**Dining areas**

Suppose you don't feel like having room service from your hotel. In that case, you can go to dining areas such as the Siglunes Restaurant serve the best Lamb Tagine, and the

Hannes Boy, which serves Cod with lobster sauce, carrots, and small fried potatoes, and you will enjoy the view of the harbor and Sigló Hotel. Adalbakari serves delightful bakery and coffee; the TORGID restaurant offers pizza, fish soup, and mashed potatoes. Fish and chips restaurant, the harbor houses that serve smoked herring, and the Fishkbou Fjallabyggoar provide the best fish and chips in the country.

●**Health care center**

You will always find health facilities near you in Siglufjordur. Some health care centers include Sjúkeahús Suglufjardar at Hvanneyrarbraut 37-39, 580 Siglufjordur, the Akureyri History at Eyrarlandsvegur, 600 Akureyri. The Heilsugæla Kópavogs at Hambraborg 8, Kópavogur. Heilbrigdisstofnunin Saudárkróki and the Salahverfi Health Care Center.

Day 2: Grimsey Island

Also called midnight sun island. Grimsey is 41km off the Iceland coast and the country's Northernmost Island. The island is secluded and windswept. The area is about 5sq km. The place is beautiful, and the only downside is that it's difficult to reach. In summer, the number of people living on the island reaches up to 100, and in winter, you will find zero to very few living on the island.

The island is the best location to watch the arch bird as you will find many bird species during summer. Aside from watching birds, there are other fun activities like visiting the famous old church, seeing the Grimsey lighthouse, eating at their local restaurants, dipping in the swimming pool, etc.

You can reach the island via ferry or airplane. The ferry from Dalvik works from the capital city on Mondays, Wednesdays, and Fridays. You will spend about three hours on the way. Alternatively, you can book a flight from Akureyri, which is about a 25-minute trip. The flights run every day in summer and only 3 days a week during the other months of the year.

If you follow the ferry, you only have five hours to explore the island after dropping off, and the ferry will take you back to the town. In winter, when daylight is shortened, the time reduces to two to four hours, so please be mindful of the scheduled times.

What can you do on Grimsey Island?

You can do several things in Grimsey: watch birds, hike, visit old buildings, go to swimming pools, eat, and lodge. In fact, you will be fascinated by how the small land offers much despite its small size.

●**Watch birds**

There are several bird species in Grimsey. The birds form a nest on the island because of the abundant fishing waters of the Arctic Sea nearby. There are no predators to reduce the number of birds, and over time the bird's egg collection has diminished. The Arctic Puffin is the most well-known bird you will see while visiting. One of the largest Puffin colonies in Iceland is here. Its Tern nesting site is one of the largest in Iceland as well. The perfect time to see the Puffin or Tern is from the end of April to the beginning of August.

As the weather gets colder, the birds migrating will leave the island to look for warmer places, and those in the ocean will head out searching for a warmer area. Several sea birds will begin to return to the island towards the end of February to find a better spot in the cliffs to nest.

●Hiking

Within 14 hours, you can walk around the entire island. You will see three hiking trails marked red, green, and yellow. Each of the hiking trails starts close to the harbor. The red path is about 5 miles long and will take about 2h 30 mins. The yellow route is shorter, about 3.8 miles long, and the green path is the quickest, at about 2.5 miles; it will take about 1H 30 mins to finish. The hiking terrain includes gravel roads, moors, tracks, and paved roads. You can visit the Arctic Circle monument that represents the area the Arctic Circle cuts through the island.

●Grimseyjarkirkja (the Grimsey Church)

In the 11th century, Jón Ögmundsson, an early Icelandic Catholic bishop, consecrated the Grimsey Church. The church was dedicated to the patron saint of Norway, St. Olaf. The current church you will see was built in 1867 and constructed from driftwood that washed onto the island shore. And in 1932, the church was later removed and extended.

The church's exterior is painted white with a reddish-brown roof. What attracts many tourists is the altar painting, a copy of Leonardo da Vinci's painting done by a local artist in 1878.

Many people visit the church and give donations for good luck. Every year, a vicar from the village of Dalvil visits the church 4 times to serve. The church is very well known and is a part of the extensive history of Grimsey.

●Swimming pool

If you want to relax your body after an active day, then the Grimsey thermal swimming pool is the place to do so. It has an outdoor pool and hot tub. The hours of operation are Mondays, Tuesdays, and Wednesdays from 8 pm to 9:30 pm and Saturdays from 2 pm to 4 pm. The pool doesn't operate on Thursdays, Fridays, and Sundays.

The entry price is 750 ISK for adults, 250 ISK for seniors, and 200 ISK for children. The contact number for the pool is 354-461-3155.

●**Dining centers**

The only place you can dine in Grimsey is the Restaurant Krían, located in the village center, opposite the harbor at Hafnargata 3, located at 611 Akureyri. From the restaurant, you will have a good view of the ocean. It's open every day in summer and occasionally during the other months of the year. The restaurant serves dishes such as fresh fish of the day and hot soups. The restaurant can accommodate up to 50 people, and the location is enhanced with a stocked bar. And if you want to try Puffin, you can find local exotic delicacies. You can contact the restaurant via 354-467-3112 or 354-898- 2058.

●**Accommodation**

You can lodge in the Guesthouse Gullsól at Sólbergi 611, Grimsey, the Guesthouse Básar near the Arctic circle, and the airport.

Day 3: Laufas Turf Homes

The Laufas Turf House is one of the biggest houses in Iceland, located in Eyjafjördur fjord in North Iceland.

The turf house is an old Icelanders settlement from 874 to 930. It's a traditional building where both the rich and poor Icelanders lived. In the olden days, turf houses were all over the country, big, small, and medium, depending on how wealthy the owner was. However, only a few of these houses are left, inherited by the past generation, which has now become a part of the tourist attractions.

The most prominent turf houses are now under the supervision of the Iceland National Museum, **Pjódminjasfnid**. You can only visit the turf houses in summer as they are usually closed in winter. And seeing these places will give you the sense that you have returned to the olden days.

From the name, the houses were built with turf and rocks and in areas where lava is available. The lava was used in the turf houses' walls. Because of their building materials, the homes require constant maintenance.

Laufás farm is an old farm that dates back to the Iceland settlement, though it wasn't mentioned in the Book of Iceland Settlements- Landñama. Laufás has several turf farms, which are being maintained and rebuilt constantly.

Laufás was rebuilt in 1866-1870 by Rev. Björn Halldórsson, who served at Laufás from 1853 to 1882. The turf house is a rich vicarage built for a minister with a big household and twenty to thirty people living there.

The last minister to live in the Laufás home was Rev. Porvadur Porma. He served as a minister at Laufás from 1927-1959. But in 1935, he left the turf home and moved to a new vicarage.

From 1957 to 1959, 1976 to 1978, 1994 to 2003, and 2009-2012, the Laufás turf house was rebuilt and renovated. Still, the oldest part dates to 1840, and the two oldest types of wood are believed to be two or more centuries older.

The turf walls are incredibly thick and have been built with an insulation system to help, especially during long and frigid winter days.

Badstofa, or living room, is the main room in the turf house where the people living there used to gather at night, eat, do handiwork, and sleep. The interior of the rooms was customarily paneled, and the inside of the turf house resembles a timber house.

What will amaze you about the turf houses is that they are bigger inside compared to how you view them from the outside. The Laufas is spacious, having multiple furnished corridors and rooms; you will also find old items from 1900. You will also see old clothes and other household items; some were collected from the neighboring farms, while some were originally in the Laufás. Beware when you enter the turf houses because it's believed that the people who lived there were smaller, so if you are tall, watch your head so you won't bump into the walls. Also, when you visit, check if you can see the carved eider duck on one of the roofs. Although it's currently broken, you might find an old photo of the eider duck from afar. You will see an eider nesting area owned by the Laufás Farm, represented by the eider duck. The word eiderdown for Laufás people means

'considerable income.'

You can buy tickets for visiting the Laufás museum from the white house at the parking space near the turf house. It was an old vicarage, now Laufás visitor's center.

●The Laufáskirkja church

Next to Laufás turf house is the unique, white-painted church, the 6th church erected at Laufás, built-in 1865. The church is a Catholic church dedicated to Apostle Paul. Inside the church, you will find the well-carved and painted pulpit that dates to 1698, and it describes the four Evangelists with Christ in the middle.

Tryggvi Gunnarsson, the son of Rev. Gunnar Gunnarsson, designed the church at Laufás from 1835 to 1917.

Day 4: Husavik

Before, Husavik was just a peaceful small town with a small appeal to the outside world. But today, it has become one of the most attractive and most-visited tourist attraction centers. It is a must-see destination, and visiting Iceland is incomplete without going to the town. Aside from the exciting activities such as whale watching, the small town has the charm to draw your attention, especially with its tasty restaurants and classic Icelander hospitality. Just make sure you give this beautiful town a visit when you go to North Iceland.

The town is home to more than 3,000 full-time residents. The number increases in summer because of tourists visiting the city and Icelanders visiting on buses to tour.

Things you can see in Husavik
 ● **Hvalasafnid á Húsavík (The Húsavík Whale Museum)**
The opening hours are June to August, 8:30 am to 6:30 pm daily; from April to May, and September, 9 am to 4 pm daily. And from October to March, 10 am to 3:30 pm from Monday to Friday, excluding weekends. The entrance fee is 1,400 ISK. The museum is comprehensive, featuring the most famous museum mammals. The exhibit was developed and maintained with great care, and the curator is passionate about whales. The extensive museum was previously a slaughterhouse. It will detail the whale species that inhibit the water of Iceland's coasts and the whale ecology and conservation.

You will find almost ten different whale skeletons, sperms, and jaw bones that reach the size of a car which is so incredible to stand next to. You will also see short films that teach about whales and a library that has a vast selection of marine-related books.

● **Könnunarsögusafnid (the Exploration Museum)**

The Exploration Museum opens daily from 9 am to 6 pm, and the entrance fee is 1,000 ISK. The museum is the best place to view something different in North Iceland. You will find many things you can focus on, such as how Vikings came to Iceland, how Americans landed on the moon, and many more. You will see maps and photographs on display and documentaries about Apollo astronauts' training in Húsavík.

● **The Húsavík culture house**

The culture house is open from 10 am to 6 pm daily from June to August, 10 am to 4 pm Monday to Friday from September to May. The entrance fee is 600 ISK. The culture house has two excellent exhibitions that have given Húsavík a window of life over the ages. The first exhibit contains a maritime theme and has boats built in Húsavík. The other display includes fishing equipment, dealing and shark hunting tools, and photos and documentaries in English. The second exhibits focus on the region's daily life and natural history. In this area, you can see homemade items and crafts and learn about farming subsistence. You will also find regional archives and a library.

● **Húsavíkkurkirkja (the Húsavík Church)**

The church was built in 1907; it is situated near the harbor. The entrance is free, and the opening hours are 9 am to 11 am and 3 pm to 5 pm daily from June to August. The church is among the known outstanding landmarks in Húsavík. It stands 26 meters high and has a whitish exterior and reddish-brown trim, the steeple dark green. The interior is made from solid wood beams, beautiful windows, and red cushioned pews. The Icelandic state architect Rögnvaldul Ólafsson designed the church, and the wood used in the construction was imported from Norway. The town locals revered the painting at the back of the altar. Sveinn Thórarinsson, the Icelandic artist, portrays the resurrection of Lazarus for the church. His work also incorporated the landscape of Iceland, the mountains, and the mist from Dettifos.

Sports activities available in Húsavík
  ● **Camping**
You can go camping in the Húsavík Campground, usually open from mid-May to mid-September, with an entrance fee

of 1,200 ISK. The place is prominent, well maintained, and has efficient facilities that are popular from June to July. It has a great kitchen area and steaming hot showers. The camping ground is close to the city town, located in an open field without shelter. You are welcome to bring tents and RVs.

● **Swimming**

You can also dip in the Húsavík swimming pool near the camping site. The opening hours are usually 9 am to 7 pm from Monday to Friday and 10 am to 5 pm on weekends. The entrance fee is 600 ISK. But the swimming pool is often crowded, so you must take extra caution, and there are a couple of hot tubs beside the pool.

● **Whale watching**

One of the best activities that tend to lead people to Húsavík is whale watching. Your visit would be incomplete if you visited but did not get on a boat to watch these giant creatures up close. The primary whale-watching season lasts from the middle of May to October, ending in June and July. During this time, you can view up to twelve different whale species. You can see the common whale species, such as the minke and humpback whales, and if you are lucky, you will also see other delicate species, like fin whales, orcas, blue whales, and sometimes even dolphins. Your guide might even tell you more about the whales and their up-close-and-personal encounters with them. Three companies run the whale-watching tours.

The Gentle Giants work from April to mid-November. Contact: 354/464-1500, entrance fee: 10,300 ISK

North sailing that works from mid-March to November. Contact: 354/464-7272. Entrance fee: 10,500 ISK.

Salka works from mid-May to mid-September. Contact: 354/464-3999. Entrance fee: 9,950 ISK.

●Dining areas

You can find many dining options that offer sumptuous delicacies, such as the Naustid, which serves seafood. The Fish and Chips restaurant is known to serve the best fish and chips in the world, the restaurant Salka serves fish soup and bread, and Gamli baukur serves risotto, fish, sweet potato fries, etc. The Heimabakari Konditori serves coffee, Lokal serves delicious gelato and coffee, and many more restaurants.

●Accommodations

Some hotels you can lodge include the Fosshotel in Ketilebraut 22, Húsavík, the Húsavík cape Hotel at Höfdi 24, Svartaborg at Útkinn 851, Rangárvegur, the Breidamyri Farm Apartments at Breidamyri, EinarsstadirLaugar, the Guesthouse Stóru - Laugar at Stóru Laugar, Laugar, etc.

Day 5: Hofsos

Hofsos is a small village in Northwest Iceland. Despite the village's small size, it offers a plethora of exciting activities that will keep you in awe and make you want to visit again. You will learn about their wellness, beautiful nature, and exciting history. The town has about 209 inhabitants. The village was a busy trading center in the 17th and 18th centuries, but despite that, it remains a small town without growing much even up to the 20th century. The village generates its economy from fishing and providing services to the neighborhood farms. Recently, the city has built itself as a tourist attraction center, thus bringing extra limelight and life to the town, especially in summer.

Things to do in Hofsos

●Swim in the infinity pool by the sea

Although the pool is small, you will still enjoy a unique view of the ocean and the mountains on the other side of Skagafjödur fjord. The small and wonderful place allows you to relax in the warm water and even chat with your traveling partner or the other people in the tub. You can check the pool's website on Facebook if you are on social media to see their schedules. The collection used to open daily from June through August and occasionally throughout the rest of the year.

●Visit Basalt Columns behind the swimming pool

The basalt column is a hidden gem behind or below the swimming pool, depending on how you see it. You can view it from the pool or the parking space. To find the place, walk towards the sea from the parking space to the left of the pool. You will see stairs, follow and find the basalt columns. You can sit on one of the columns and snap beautiful pictures. Note: be careful while walking down the shore and climbing the coast so you won't get hurt.

●Check the Icelandic Emigration Center

The Icelandic Emigration Center is one of the best places in North Iceland, where you will find some fascinating history of Iceland. You will read the story of the people who emigrated from Iceland to North America in the late 19th and the beginning of the 20th century. History estimated that around sixteen to twenty thousand people emigrated from Iceland to North America in search of a better life. This number is enormous, equating to about 20-25% of the total Iceland population at that time. The vast majority of those who moved indicated Iceland's living conditions were too challenging. There were harsh weather conditions that added to natural disasters that led to economic hardship, forcing them to migrate. Thanks to the people who still stayed, if all of them had decided to leave at that time, the country would cease to exist, and we would not have to change to appreciate its natural scenery.

●Walk around to explore the village

To the West of Hofsos is a beautiful ocean view, and to the East is a mighty mountain. You can also view the mountain from the west, just that it is a little farther. The fascinating part of the town is down by the harbor. The place around the Emigration Center. In that area, you will see beautiful old houses which. Some belong to the center, one is a restaurant, and the rest belong to other people.

There is a beautiful restaurant that serves sumptuous meals, usually open in summer, the patio there is fantastic, and you will enjoy a good ocean view from there. What makes Hofsos a must-visit location is how uncrowded it is. It is far from the busy tourist centers so the atmosphere will be pleasant and relaxing.

But, since the town is small, few people visit it, so the good restaurants there will have a tough time surviving; thus, they only open during high seasons.

●Visit Grafarkirkja

Close to Hofsos is Grafarkirkja, the oldest church in Iceland. The church is located 5 km/ 3m from Hofsos. The church is in the middle of a field surrounded by towering mountains in the background. It also has a beautiful frame of circular turf wall. The church is no longer open to the public for personal reasons, so you cannot enter. So, although you can only view it from the outside, it's still worth visiting.

●Go to the Grettislaug Hot spring

You can soak in the Grettislaug Hot Spring near the sea.

●Dining centers

Some dining centers in Hofsos include the Veitingastofsn Solvik restaurant that serves fantastic fish and chips, the Lonkot Rural Resort, the Retro Mathus, and the newly opened Berg Bistro.

●Accommodations

You can lodge in any of these accommodations. The Sunnuberg Guesthouse at Sudurbraut 8 Hofsos, Fraendqardur at Kvosin Hofsos, the Matti Guesthouse at Sudurbraut 1 Hofsos, or the Kolkuós Guesthouse at Kolkuós Hofsos.

Day 6: Dalvik

Iceland's striking beauty can never be overemphasized; the seaside and fishing villages in the county look as if they are straight out of a postcard. Dalvik is a small town in North Iceland; the name Dalvik means **'Valley Bay.'**

Things to do in Dalvik

●Visit Gísli, Eiríkur, Helgi Cafe

The Café is one of the best spots you can visit in Dalvik. It's one of the town's favorites, owned by Heldur and Bjarni, who are exceptionally hospital hosts and will make you feel as if you are at home. They also own a hostel and schools on the street. They are interesting people that will make your visit lively, their children are a fixture of the local scene, and Bjarni is famous for his storytelling. Another aspect that makes the place fascinating is that it has a quick decor, and from upstairs, you can have a stunning view of the sea. You can enjoy coffee, tea, beer, or hot chocolate. They serve a tasty fish soup with three different homemade pieces of bread.

●Visit Buggdasafnid Hvoll Folk Muhistory to learn the Icelandic History

Go to the Icelandic museum to learn about the culture and heritage of Dalvík. You will see a lot of unusual collections of objects and artifacts. You will find many surprising items, such as a stuffed polar bear. You will see many odds and ends from the Icelandic culture of patrimony. You will see rooms that tell the story of Jóhann K. Pétursson, who was known we the Icelandic Giant, Iceland's tallest man measuring 2.34m (7ft, 8 inches), and you will find how he fascinated most of the shorter Icelanders.

●Go skiing and snowboarding in winter

Dalvik is located in the Svarfadardalur valley, which makes it one of the best skiing, snowboarding, and other winter sports locations. Böggvisstadafjall mountain, situated in Dalvik, has top-rated facilities. It has 5 km of slopes, including a 1,200m flood fit run. There are also bunny slopes for the less seasoned skiers. Recently, they produced a new snow production system that keeps fresh powder coming. The ski resort isn't far from the town, so it's easier for you to walk around.

●Watch birds

The town is close to mountains and famous for its high bird population. Just pack your lunch from Samkaup Úrval, the town's central market, and go to the hills. If you go there in late May and June, you will see all the migrant birds. To impress the locals with your little Icelandic bird species knowledge, shout the famous Icelandic phrase **'Lóan er komin,'** which means **'the Golden Plover has arrived.'**

●Hiking

Aside from watching birds, you can also hike in the mountains.

●Watch Whales

One of the first things that will attract your attention when you visit Dalvik is the diversity of Iceland's flora and fauna. The country is an island nation with a fantastic plethora of marine life. You will see the attractive Atlantic puffin who returns to land to breed colonies. The Icelandic waters contain seven species of dolphins, including the black and white orca. But this isn't the unique aspect of Dalvik; what makes it more remarkable is looking for the ocean's most giant mammals submerged under the surface of the icy waters. Dalvik is the best destination to watch Whales because it's located in the eastern part of the Tröllaskagi Peninsula. Just imagine how beautiful it will be to see one of these majestic creatures jumping and splashing down from the Norwegian sea.

●**Watch the Dalvík Fiskidagurinn Mikli Fish Festival**

Just prepare your taste buds because, in Dalvík, you will eat all sorts of fish free during their fish festival. The festival is a daylong activity where you can eat a free seafood buffet, and amazingly everyone is invited to partake of the offerings. The local fishing industry sponsors the day, so everyone can enjoy what Iceland is famously known for (Herring.) If you happen to travel to North Iceland in summer, the first or second week of August, check North Iceland's calendar; the festival day is one of the highlights of summer. In any month of the year, you visit Dalvík, you will find the town worth visiting with many fun activities waiting for you. Dalvík is just 35 minute drive from Akureyri.

●**Dining areas**

You can eat at restaurants such as the Bjorbordin spa, which offers a spa session and restaurant, and you can eat meals and beer-related foods. Gregor's restaurant serves lamb, Cod, salmon, etc. The Baccala bar serves freshly caught fish: Nurdur restaurant and many more.

●**Accommodations**

You can lodge in any of the following hotels. The Brekkusel Lodge at XC9V+FQP, Skidabraut, 620 Dalvík. The Dalvík hostel at Grundargata, 620 Dalvík. Hotel Dalvík at Skidabraut 18, 620 Dalvík.

Day 7: Asbyrgi Canyon

The Asbyrgi canyon, translated as The **Shelter of Gods,** is a hidden gem situated in North Iceland, part of the Vatnajökull national park. Has the shape of a giant horseshoe bend with steep cliffs.

There are two ways you can leverage the Asbyrgi canyon.

1. By hiking up the canyon cliffs to view the horseshoe from above
2. Or by walking down the stairs to enjoy the canyon valley and lake Botnstjorn.

If you choose option one, know that hiking can take up to three to four hours, and it requires energy though it's a sight to behold. Option two is much easier and less time-consuming. You can drive past the visitor center into the canyon towards the lake, park, and walk around. The downside of option two is that the view is less spectacular compared to option one. The last part of the canyon is the Asbyrgi; before you reach there, you will see a long rock formation of the canyon known as Eylan between East and West.

●**The visitor center**

The best place to park your vehicle if you plan to hike the canyon wall or the long canyon valley is the visitor center Gjúrfrastofa. You will see a big map outside. Inside the visitor center, you will find people that will tell you where to go. You will see different routes; follow the one you are interested in. Also, in the Jökulsárgljúfur area is a small museum about flora and fauna. The visitor center opening hours in July and August is between 11h to 17h daily, and during the other months, it opens and closes 1-2h later or earlier and only from Mondays to Fridays. There are no eating items for sale in the visitor center, you can only fill your water bottles for free in the restrooms, and you must pay camping fees.

How to climb the canyon

●The longer route

Suppose you have the energy to follow the steep stairs and ropeway; welcome. Follow left past the visitor center and the gold course on your right side after walking for about 5 to 10 mins. You will see a wooden gate, and shortly after you pass the gates, you will see signs of a wooden path. Follow the Vesturdalur sign at your right and walk to the gorge wall. You will first walk through grassland; the passage will continue between low trees and bushes. Follow the canyon edge by your right and walk the path for like 1.6 km, which goes higher and higher. You will sometimes see steep stairs with ropes on your right side. Continue walking; keep following the edge of the canyon by your right for like 4 km.

●On the Top

Once you reach the tip, walking on the canyon's wall is flat. You have to climb up and down a few rocks once in a while. You will mainly walk through a narrow way in a fine rocky field. Watch your steps to avoid tripping over the rocks or tree roots that stick out of the ground, especially when coming back tired.

After about 1 hour of walking, you will reach a place with a beautiful view. You can also look past the rock wall in the middle of the canyon and the valley on both sides. The view is stunning and fascinating. Even if you stop here, you have at least had a unique experience, but the most beautiful scenery is yet to come; you still have a 30-minute walk to reach there.

●Earthquake

After the 25 mins walk, start climbing more. You will reach a substantial natural platform edge, a beautiful sight to hold, and a photography area. But this area is now closed with safety ribbons to warn tourists. The recent earthquake caused deep cracks that made it dangerous to walk to the edge. Further, walk for 5 minutes, and you will be welcome with a beautiful view of the canyon walls and the sky up close. This is your reward for walking for one and a half hours despite its challenges.

Day 8: Dettifos Waterfall

Dettifoss is one of the fantastic waterfalls in North Iceland. The waterfall is known for its size, not appearance; it's the second most powerful waterfall in Europe that will give you a spectacular and breathtaking view when you visit it. It measures 45 meters high and 100 meters wide. The waterfall is sometimes referred to as 'The Beast' of Godafoss. The water came from Jökulsa á Fjöllom, the glacier river that flows from the most significant ice cap in Europe, the Vatnajökull glacier. Dettifoss water is rich in sediment and flows and reaches the Greenland Sea. The term Dettifos means **'The collapsing waterfall.'** You will understand why it's named this when you stand before it.

How to reach the waterfall
You can drive and reach the waterfall, although the road conditions and access depend on the weather and season. Whenever you are going, make sure you drive the right car and check the road conditions.

The drive from Akureyri to Dettifoss is about two hours, and if you are coming from Reykjavik (the capital of Iceland), the drive can take up to seven hours. You will follow the Ring Road to reach the waterfall and then take the detour. You can get the waterfall from two sides, and two roads lead to the viewing center.

●Road 862

If you follow Road 862, a paved road suitable for cars, it will take you to the western side of the waterfall. The road is open from April to December. If you are arriving from Asbyrgi, you will reach the waterfall in about 30mins, and if you are coming from Reykjavik, the drive is about 40 mins.

●Road 864

Road 864 will drive you to the eastern part of the waterfall. The road is usually open from May ending to the beginning of October. It's closed during winter because of the hazardous weather. This road is gravel with many potholes and uneven trains, so drive slowly and carefully.

The best side of Dettifoss Waterfall

The Western side is easier to drive because the paved 862 road is accessible for all vehicles. This side shows a golden hour light in all seasons, making it the best photography point. Most people follow road 862 to reach the waterfall. That is why it has a new and ample parking space. After getting to the waterfall, you will need to walk small before you reach the waterfall. There is an easy hiking part.

The best time to visit Dettifoss Waterfall

What you will experience when you visit depends on the season you go there. The waterfall is at its peak in summer, with an average water flow of 400m³/s. The best time to visit Dettifoss if you want a scenic experience is June through

August.

If you visit in summer, it is also an enjoyable experience but overcrowded. Summer is a high season when most people choose to visit tourist centers. And if you visit in summer but do not want to come across the crowd, it is best to go in the late afternoon.

If you visit in winter, you will be welcomed by snowy and frozen landscapes with a beautiful view. In winter, the daylight hours are minimal, and the waterfall is not illuminated in the darkness. So, plan your visit at this time of the year. Road 864 is closed in winter because of heavy snow and mud and does not open until May or Early June.

Things to do or see near Dettifoss Waterfall

You can go to many landmarks during your visit to Dettifoss Waterfall, such as

●**The Selfoss Waterfall**

Selfoss is also a waterfall close to Dettifoss on the river Jökulsa á Fjöllum. Even though the waterfall is less powerful and significant than Dettifos, Selfoss still has a beautiful appearance. Moreover, it is comprehensive and has multiple smaller waterfalls. Both the two waterfalls share the same parking space, and it only takes a 30-minute hike from Dettifoss Waterfall to reach Selfoss. To reach Selfoss, it is best to follow Road 864 because you will have a better view from the Eastern side. Though you can take the western side there, you can only view it from another perspective.

●**Hafragilsfoss**

Hafragilsfoss is smaller than Selfoss and Dettifos Waterfalls. But it is still worth visiting. Cliffs surround Hafragilsfoss, and its waterfall is thirty meters high and ninety meters wide. From this waterfall, you can have a beautiful view of the Jökulsárgljúfur canyon. The eastern side is the main place to have the best view of this waterfall. You can also view it from the western side; abide by the indications from Dettifoss Waterfall.

Tips for visiting Dettifoss
- Be sure the road is in good condition before driving.
- Have spare tires or winter tires and drive carefully in winter. The roads can be icy and with gravel.
- Rent a 4×4 car if you plan to reach Dettifos from the East side.
- The parking space is free
- If you are not visiting alone, consider going in the evening.
- Bring waterproof shoes and outer layers.

Day 9: Lake Myvatn

Lake Myvatn is a particular area in North Iceland, the fourth-largest water body in Iceland. It features beautiful geographical landmarks, rich flora and fauna, and multiple impressive sites surrounding it. The lake is among the Diamond Circle Highlights, famous Iceland's travel route.

You can only find a small town in Lake Myvatn called Reykjavik. In the city, you can find necessities like a gas station, bank, mini supermarket, restaurant, Guesthouse health-care center, school, etc.
- **The Golden Circle**
Lake Myvatn is part of Diamond Circle, a sightseeing road

linked to Húsavík, Asbyrgi Canyon, and Dettifoss Waterfall. The lake region completes the Diamond Circle Road, and the other features do not overshadow it. You can do plenty of activities there, such as birdwatching, fishing, and relaxing in the nature baths.

Tips for visiting Lake Myvatn
- Explore from your car; you will have the best sight.
- Wear your hiking shoes
- Add 30 minutes extra time if you want to experience the lake area. Drive around the area to have a complete view.
- When you drive the lake's full perimeter, you will view multiple landscapes that make an excellent photography point.
- Carry along a mosquito net, use insect repellent, or wear long sleeves.

The best time to visit Lake Myvatn

The lake changes with the season. For example, you will find it bright and vibrant, with abundant wildlife and birdlife in summer. While you will find winter quiet and peaceful, the colors are replaced with frosty whites and blues.

Places you can lodge close to Myvatn Lake

You can lodge in any of the following inns—the Fosshotel Myvatn, Hotel Laxa, Icelandair Hotel Myvatn, Sel-Hotel Myvatn, etc.

Day 10: Godafoss waterfall

The Godafoss waterfall is among the fascinating sights in North Iceland. It is located off the rind road, so make sure you visit this beautiful place when passing through the ring road. The name Godafoss means **'waterfall of Gods.' There** are even people that believe that the waterfall is God-like in beauty. However, an old legend in Iceland gives the tale of the waterfall's name through a Viking leader named Porgeir Ljósvetningagodi. The name Porgeir resulted from his throwing his pagan statues into the waterfall. The actual story of the waterfall is not really known, so it's better to leave it as a mystery and thus make it mythic.

The waterfall is among the largest ice waterfalls in Iceland and is considered to be one of Iceland's genuine pearls. The river Skjálfandafjót feeds the river and runs in a 7000-year-old lava field from the Trölladyngja volcano. The word troll is the troll word you know in English, so we can say the area is mystical. Most of Iceland's folklore tales take it as inspiration.

Godafoss flows 30-meter-wide horseshoe-shaped rock and rises in the center, which separates the waterfall into two. The first section is 9m, and the second is seventeen meters.

Godafoss location

Godafoss is in the Northern part of Iceland, off ring road 1. It is 438km from Reykjavik, 214km from Egilsstadir, and 50km from Akureyri. The closest attraction near Godafoss waterfall is the Geitafoss waterfall. The Godafoss GDF coordinates are

65.6828 °N, 17. 5502 °W.

How to reach the Godafoss waterfall

Godafoss waterfall is marked well with a big sign, and it will be hard for you to miss the location. There is a beautiful parking space located west of the waterfall. Most people visit the waterfall while driving along the ring road or visiting North Iceland.

Places to lodge near Godafoss waterfall

If you plan to visit Godafoss more than once or want to lodge near the waterfall, here are some accommodations options.

1. Hotel Edda Stórutjarnir
2. Hotel Laugar
3. Guesthouse Fosshól
4. Fljótsbakki farm
5. Vallakot farm Guesthouse
6. North Aurora Guesthouse
7. Einishus cottages
8. Kjarnagedi cottages, etc.

Areas to camp near Godafoss

Near Godafoss are plenty of camping grounds. The price for a night ranges from 1200 to 2000 ISK. The camping grounds are well equipped with facilities.

● **The Guesthouse Fosshóll**

The Guesthouse is the closest camping ground to Godafoss, just five hundred meters away. The camping grounds offer running water, toilets, gas stations, a restaurant, and a grocery shop. The Guesthouse is usually open from 15th May to 15th September.

● Hild at Myvatn

This camping group is open all year round and is just 1km away from lake Myvatn. The camping ground will provide you with toilets, electricity, a cooking tent, a playground, and a small shop.

● Systragril

It is located in the fertile Fnjoskadalur valleys, a few steps away from the Vaglaskógur forest. They offer a spot for cooking, heated bathrooms, washers, showers, a golf course, fishing, a swimming pool, and a playground. It is usually open from early June to October 30th.

● Vaglaskógur

This place offers toilets, hot and cold water, walking paths, showers, electricity, a golf course, and a playground.

Things to note before you visit Godafoss waterfall

● You can enjoy a sumptuous meal in a restaurant a few minutes away from the waterfall while simultaneously having a beautiful view of the waterfall.

● You can visit a lot of places from Godafoss waterfall

● Make sure to visit the waterfall from both sides, and you will experience a wholly unique perspective of the waterfall.

● Watch your steps while walking because the rocks near the waterfall are slippery.

Chapter 3

Unique destinations to go from day 11 to day 20

Day 11: Dimmuborgir Lava Formations

The Dimmuborgir is a dark fortress at Myvatn with true natural wonder. It contains vast lava rock formations that make you feel like you are on another planet. Call it a fairy tale world. The lava pillar formation originated from molten lava, which created a lava pond in the eruption of Lúdentarborgir and Prengslaborgir row of craters around 2,300 years ago.

The molten lava started to solidify on the surface resulting in a crusty roof; the lava flow then deepened the lava pond. The water on the ground then became trapped under the lava pond; steam started coming out through the vent, which created the lava and formed those pillars. The solidified posts can keep standing even after the lava pond empties and the lava roof has collapsed. This phenomenon is often referred to as Hraubóla or lava bubble. Because of their formation process, the rocks are brittle and fragile, so they cannot climb them.

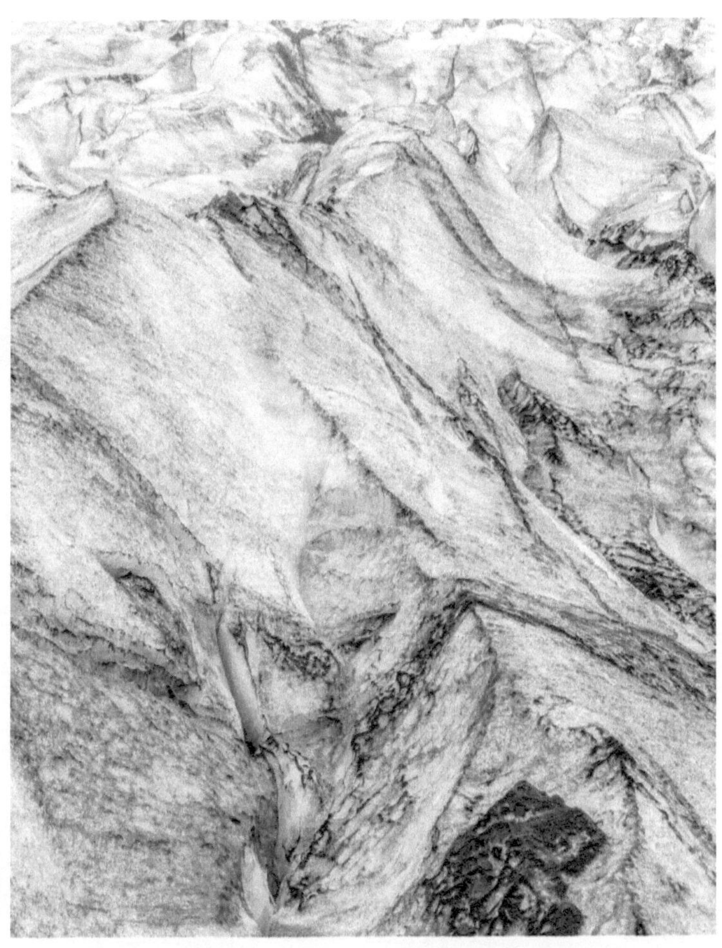

You will find plenty of bird species in the lava that don't like disturbance, such as the Falcon, so it's best to follow the paths and avoid walking on the roped-in areas of the vegetation. The size of Dimmuborgir is about 1-2 km in diameter and 20 meters in height. It has plenty of walking paths; make sure you follow the color of the road you choose. Some of the lava looks exactly the same, so it can be easy for you to lose, leaving you thinking, "I have been here before."

●**Kirkjan**

Kirkjan is a church at Dimmuborgir. Among the roads you will find in the lava is the one that leads to this church. The church is about 2.4 km, and it can take one hour to reach the church. The path to the church will take you through an extraordinarily tall formation for an hour before you reach the church.

You will see a sign that says KIRKJA and the best-known lava formation. Walking to the church, you will see a cave that opens at both ends with a high domed-shaped roof. The cave looks artificial, but it is a lava cave that resembles a Gothic church. Remember, the entrance to Dimmuborgir's name is **Borgarás.** While coming back, you will walk through sand hills and close the ring by the parking space. The route is marked well, so it will be hard for you to lose unless you follow a different path at dark.

●**The Jólasveinahellirinn (Cave of the Yule Lads)**

There is a hidden gem located in Dimmuborgir that everyone does not know about; the cave where the Icelandic Yule Lads lived. There are 13 Yule Lads in Iceland, which are different from Santa Claus. There are also more than 70 Yule Lad names recorded, but these thirteen are famous because they stayed with Icelanders until the modern era. They were raised by two trolls, Gryla and Leppalúdi; though they were not as bad as their parents, they were still ill-mannered. Though, who wouldn't be ill-mannered after being raised by trolls?

The Yule is rarely seen outside in summer as they are inside their cave resting or sleeping. But it's a different story in November and December; if you go there at this time of the year, there is a high chance that you might run into the mischievous Yule Lad. Around 13 days before Christmas, the first Yule Lad will come to inhabited areas, and another one will arrive every day until the last lad arrives on the 24th of December. Their cave is strangely formed, and you will find lava beds belonging to each Yule Lad and their other personal items. If they do not come back and see you in their cave, you can roam around a little and even go through their things. There is a kitchen inside the cave; you will also see their laundry hung up to dry. Just try and leave the cave on time because they might pop up at any moment.

Though it is hard to find the cave, you will see that it is worth it when you locate it. If you cannot find this cafe and you seriously want to see the Yule Lads, there is another cave in Hallarflöt, there you might see them frequently, and the cave is easier to find though smaller than the Jólasveinahellirinn. You will see items kike small chairs and their other belongings. You will see a donation box in the cave; the box is for collecting pajama money for their father, Leppalúdi. You will also find a Yule Lads chair where you can sit and snap memorable pictures.

●**The View-Dial at Dimmuborgir**

At the Dimmuborgir parking lot, you will see a fine View-Dial designed by Jakob Hálfdanarson and erected by Náttúruverdarrád, Skútusdahreppur rural district, and Landgrædslan in 1990. Náttúruverdarrád has been making View-Dials for a decade in Iceland, and before him, his uncle Jón Vidis was in the View-Dial business.

View-Dials stand shiny and bright as if they have been newly erected. And although Iceland's harsh weather can damage the chrome on the View-Dial in Dimmuborgir, it does not affect it. The View-Dials are helpful as they show the names of the mountains in the area. At Dimmuborgir, the View-Dials are beautifully standing on top of an octagon wooden podium with a stat; it is a molten cylindrical chrome plate containing a time of three hours.

Day 12: Krafla Viti Crater

The Krafla Viti Crater is a good hiking place with excellent features for you to see that are worth your time and resources. Krafla Viti Crater is in Lake Myvatn. The word Krafla Viti means **'hell.'** It was named Viti after the violent eruptions that occurred during its formation. The explosion's aftermath left a deep crater which is now filled with water from the present-day Viti Crater Lake.

A lot of people sometimes confuse the Krafla Viti Crater with Viti Lake. They are two different entities though all geothermal features in North Iceland. Viti Lake is situated close to Askaja, and because it has hot springs, which Krafla Viti Crater lacks, people often go there instead.

●The violent volcanic eruption at Krafla

Since the ninth century, the Krafla has erupted twenty-nine times, devastatingly affecting the site. One of the most violent eruptions recalled occurred between 1724 and 1729. People will never forget it due to how high the lava and rocks were thrown from the volcano. Even people from the southern part of Iceland can see the lava flow. This occurrence was later referred to as **Myvatn Fires.**

Happily, no casualties were reported during the event; it

only affected farms and made them lava fields for which the whole country is now known. Other recent violent eruptions happened between 1975 to 1985.

A total of nine magma eruptions were recorded during the event, but fortunately, no casualties were reported. It only damaged farms that were rendered useless for many years. The farmers left the area because it affected even the surrounding soils. The effect also affected North Iceland's tourism business for almost seven years. Though the site is now active, visitors are always warned to be careful at the place because of possible Geothermal activity.

Why you should visit the Krafla Viti Crater Lake

There are multiple reasons you should visit this area whenever you are in North Iceland. First, the Crater is uniquely surreal. You will experience an apocalypse atmosphere with the blue water surrounding the colorful mountains and the hot streams coming out of the steep walls. The Crater is enormous and stretches about three hundred meters in diameter. Its blue water makes it stunning though what you will see varies depending on the time you visit.

But as long as you stay in the Krafla fissures for some time, you will notice the color changes. Also, where you stand determines how you will see the water. Some people see aqua blue; some see turquoise blue, and others see turquoise green. You can spend days hiking in the Krafla Viti Crater, and from there, you can access Lake Myvatn.

Things you can do in the Viti Crater Lake

One of the benefits of the lake is that it is a sightseeing and adventure location. You will have the best hiking experience there. You start hiking from the parking space since that's the trailhead's beginning. The Crater is circular so that you can rim hike in any direction. It will take you about one hour to finish walking the lake. If you want to have all the lakes to yourself, go bottom.

And to have the best experience, go to the bottom of the caldera. It takes a little effort to ascend down, and you do not have to worry about returning. Though it is tiresome, you will find it a good experience. After experiencing the blue water at the Krafla Viti Crater Lake bottom, you can see some hot water by hiking to the spring. Make your next stop at the Krafla Power Station. It is a Geothermal power plan that is open for visitors to tour. There, you can learn about the unrivaled geothermal power production of the Icelandic system. The last place you should visit should be the Leirhnjúkur Lava Field. You will enjoy seeing the Icelandic geothermal activity, the largest magma-covered fields, and the bubbling mud globally.

How to reach the Krafla Viti Crater
There is no public transport that will take you to Krafla. You can only get there by bus or a private car. From Akureyri, it will take like two hours to reach Krafla.

Cafes and restaurants near the Krafla Viti Crater Lake
After you tour the Lake, you might be tired and need some refreshments. Near the lake, you can find some excellent restaurants and cafes that serve European cuisines in friendly services, such as

●The Vogafjos Cowshed Café
●The Kaffi Borgir
●Daddi's pizza
●Gamli Bistro
●Café Kvika

Hotels close to the Krafla Viti Crater Lake

You might want to spend a few days exploring the Krafla Viti Crater Lake and its areas. So, in this case, you have to stay for the night. And luckily, around the Krafla Viti Crater Lake, you will find hotels that are a few minutes drive away, such as

●The Del Hótel Mývatn
●The Eldá Guesthouse
●The Icelandair Hotel Myvatn
●The Dimmuborgir Guesthouse
●The Skútudtadir Guesthouse.

Day 13: Akureyri

Akureyri is the second largest city in Iceland, with a population of about 17,000. The city is known for its cultural education and outdoor activities. So, imagine the fun you will enjoy in this big city.

Popular tourists attraction centers in Akureyri
●The Akureyrarkirkja

This is a high-perched church in the city designed by the famous architect Gudjon Samúelsson. He was the one that also shaped the Hallgrímskirkja in Reykjavík. The church was built in 1940 and housed a remarkable 3200-pipe organ. The most striking feature that will keep you in awe about the church is the central-stained glass window above the altar, which once adored Coventry Cathedral in England before it was heavily damaged during an air raid. There is also a suspended ship hanging on the ceiling that represents the old Nordic tradition of giving offerings for fisherman's protection at sea.

●The Arctic Botanical Garden

The unique sense of tranquility will attract your attention when you visit the Arctic Botanical Garden in North Iceland. Another added benefit is the extreme location of the garden,

50 km only South of the Arctic Circle.

It is one of the most known botanical gardens in the world. You will see a beautiful blend of Arctic plants and plants from the temperate zones, and some species even manage to grow and survive in the high mountains. The garden houses more than 7,000 species of plants. The garden becomes an enchanting wonderland in winter due to snow bending the trees. Imagine yourself flocking snow buntings.

●**Dip in the local swimming pool**

The pool is located a short walk from the city center. What is a better way of enjoying your visit than doing. as the Akureyringur usually do; dip yourself in the pool after a long day of fun and sightseeing?

The pool also features two outdoor pools, pummeling water jets, water slides, a splash pool, an indoor pool, hotspots, a paddling pool, steam baths, sunbathing area, etc. Just get ready to be spoiled by the fantastic nature of this beautiful city. The entrance fee to the pool is 1000 ISK for adults and 250 ISK for kids between 6 to 17 years old.

●**Buy ice cream from Brynjuís**

What better way to have fun than taking ice cream after swimming? Brynjuís offer the best cream in the whole of the country. And availability is often limited, so you must order early. And beware, as it is often imitated, though, it can never be duplicated. What makes this ice cream the best is the unique recipe that has never changed since 1939. They serve milky ice cream covered with all sorts of toppings and tempting dips you can never find anywhere.

●Visit Iceland's Northernmost 18-hole golf course, Jadar.

This golf course's natural setting makes it attractive and stands out, among others. It is located in the middle of the countryside and offers an extensive palette of shrubs and vegetation. Some golfers had experienced the beauty and happiness of midnight golf before the Akureyri Golf Club started its annual Arctic Open Golf Tournament, which allows golfers from all over the world to gather at Summer Solstice for round-the-clock golf, providing an unforgettable view of the sun mirroring in the fjord.

●Visit the Kjarnaskógur woodland area

The woodland is located at Akureyri south, and it contains a vast range of short hiking trails and great playgrounds for your family. Millions of trees from varied species were planted within the last fifty years, providing an enormous recreational area of around 600 hectares. The woodland offers lighted and backcountry trails and an exciting 10 km long designed mountain bike trail. Since winter brings a lot of changes, the forest is designed so that you will still have a relaxed experience despite the weather. You can enjoy two playgrounds, a volleyball course, picnic areas, barbecue facilities, bird watching, etc.

●Visit the Christmas house, Jólagarðurinn

The Christmas house is just 10 minutes drive from Akureyri. A view of a bright red gingerbread house believed to be Santa's house will welcome you. You will also be welcome with a fire crackling in the fireplace and Christmas carols and mind-blowing scents. The place is open all year round, so that you can visit it at any time. Another thing that will charm you is the Christmas decorations selections and the traditional handicrafts items. Visit the garden around the house and extend your magical visit. You will see the most extensive Advent calendar hiding in a mini-dungeon.

●Soak in a beer spa

This is one of the reasons you want to visit Akureyri. Soaking in a beer spa. Scientists have proved that beer spa has natural health benefits. After soaking, you can go next door and taste the Kaldi beer. The beer spa offers many services; you can choose outdoor hot tubs, saunas, or the regular geothermal heated pools that provide panoramic views of the Hrísey island, mountains, and the Porbalds valley.

●Visit Kaffi Kú

Have you ever sneaked behind the scenes of a cowshed? Yes, right? But how often? Kaffi Kú is a cowshed owned by Sesselja and Einar, who have opened their doors for tourists to come and share their passion for animals, especially cows. The place has a restaurant where you dine while enjoying what is happening on the farm and witness farming activities such as milking and cow massage. You will be rewarded with a glass of fresh milk and greeted by the calves.

●Ski on the Hlidarfjall Slopes

Just 10 minutes from Akureyri, the Hlidarfjall Slopes are among the skiing areas in North Iceland. The days in these mountains are unforgettable despite your skiing skill level, whether you are a beginner, experienced skier, or snowboarder. Imagine fresh powder, groomed cross-country tracks, and exciting ski slopes. The ski slopes' elevation ranges from 500m to 1000m above sea level, giving you the best snow supply in water and a beautiful view of the Eyjafjördur, Greenland Sea, and Herdubred. You will want to spend all your days there.

●Hike the Súlur Mountain

Your trip to North Iceland is incomplete if you do not hike up to the peaks of Akureyri guardian, Mount Súlur. It rises above the town and features a famous marked trail to the summit of around five to six hours back and forth. Though it is not an easy hike, when you do it, you will find that it is worth it. What will welcome you from the top is a gorgeous view of Akureyri and Eyjafjördur bay, along with the mountain ranges from all sides. The mountain is primarily made of volcanic materials such as rhyolite, and it dates to the volcano eruptions that happened more than nine million years ago.

●Dive and explore the hydrothermal chimney (the Stryan chimney)

The chimney is the only accessible chimney you will find in this world. This place is considered one of the best-kept natural wonders in the North Atlantic Ocean. The chimney is the only available one discovered so far (found at 2000 to 6000 m depth) that you can scuba dive in. Though if you are an amateur in diving, it's best if you don't take yourself here because it's an adventure that requires people with advanced diving skills, and even those with the skills need a guide as the place is highly protected. The chimney rises from 65m to 15m and is still forming in some locations, and the freshwater from it is more than 11 000 years old.

●Go whale watching

You will never get tired of whale watching in North Iceland. Moreover, the country is known for its diverse wildlife and ocean creatures. Though you might watch Whales from Húsavík since it is the event's capital, you might want to experience another adventure here in Akureyri. The whale-watching tour usually departs from Hjalteyri, a well-kept secret of Eyjafjördur.

●Go horse riding in Skjaldadvík

This breathtaking place can make you forget where you are and what you are doing. The Skjaldadvík is a cozy family-run guesthouse that operates various activities for visitors. To have the best experience in the surrounding, ride the horse along the coast and inland.

●Dining areas

Since Akureyri is the center of North Iceland and among the highest populated cities in the country, you should expect many dining areas serving sumptuous meals that will keep your taste buds craving for more. You can dine in restaurants such as the Centrum Kitchen and Bar at Hafnarstæti 102, 600, and 600 Akureyri.

The Striking restaurant at Skipagata 14, 600 Akureyri. The Muhlenberg Bistro and Bar at Hafnarstæti 89,600 Akureyri. The Bautinn restaurant at Hafnarstæti is 92,600 Akureyri. The Taste Restaurant at Ràdhustorg 1,600 Akureyri. The Rub23 Restaurant at Kaupvangsstræti 6,000 Akureyri, etc.

●Accommodations

You can lodge in any of the following inns. The Akureyri HI hostel at 603, Stórholt 1, Akureyri. Saeluhus Apartments and houses at Sunnutröd 2,600 Akureyri. Akureyri Backpackers at Hafnarstræti 98,000 Akureyri. Guesthouse Akureyri at Hafnarstræti 108, 000 Akureyri. Guesthouse Sólgardar at Brekkugata 6,600 Akureyri. Icelandair Hotel Akureyri at þingvallastræti 23,600, etc.

●Health Care centers

The Akureyri Health Care Clinic at Hafnarstæti 99,600 Akureyri.

Day 14: Myvatn Nature Baths

Myvatn Nature Baths are located off the Ring Road. It is a heated pool and is among the top of North Iceland's attractive sites. The watercolor there is blue and rich in silica. It also features fantastic facilities, a sauna, and the best settings. Bathing in the pool is one of the rooted Icelandic cultures, so imagine how good it will be to have a new experience. There is a natural hot pool, a swimming pool, and a spa.

Why you should visit the Myvatn Nature Baths

Maybe you have heard of the baths before your trip to North Iceland; you will find their existence in publications related to North Iceland. Moreover, it is considered a cheaper alternative to Blue Lagoon on Reykjanes Peninsula. The blue lagoon is one of the famous hot pools in Iceland and is among the top tourist attraction centers.

What you should know about the Myvatn Nature Baths

The Myvatn Nature Baths is an artificial lagoon. If you are unaware, it does not in any way look artificial. The hot pool's setting is a barren landscape, with blue water with abundant silica and other minerals, hot water for swimming, and newly built facilities like a sauna. If you combine all these, it will make your visit an unforgettable one. The nature baths are a small drive from Lake Myvatn and near the Hverir Geothermal Area.

Although the people around the place usually bath in the area for thousands of years, Myvatn Nature Bath opened in 2004. Since then, the baths have become a vital gem to North Iceland. The entrance fee to Myvatn Nature Baths is 5900 ISK for adults. The opening hours vary depending on the season. It is open from 10 am to 11 pm from 1st June to 31st August and the rest of the year, from 12 pm to 9:30 pm. One advantage of closing the pool late is that after spending an entire day on the road, you can relax afterward.

How the visit to Myvatn Nature Baths looks like

●The parking space

When you reach the Nature Baths, the thing that will welcome you at the entrance is a space where you can park your vehicle. After you park your car in the area, you can straight work to the building in your front.

●Check-In

You will show your ticket to a receptionist inside a small front desk.

●Changing rooms

You will find men's and women's changing rooms with lockers. Select an empty safe and put your belongings in.

How to reach the Myvatn Nature Baths

The simplest way to reach the Nature Baths is by car. And the nearest town to the Nature Baths is Reykjahlid, Lake Myvatn shores.

●By a car

Getting to the Myvatn Nature Baths by car is super easy. From Egilsstadir, follow road 1 for 160 km. Turn left to the paved access road and drive for 3 km before Reykjahlid.

The best time to visit Myvatn Nature Baths

Though the Nature Baths are open all year round, the best time to visit is in summer. Summer months are naturally warmer, and it is okay even if it rains.

Hotels near the Myvatn Nature Baths

Many travelers used to stay overnight, so there are multiple comfortable hotels nearby, such as the Grimstunga guesthouse, the Fosshotel Myvatn, the Fosshótel Húsavík, the Gistihusid Lake hotel Egilsstadir, the Centrum Guesthouse, etc.

Day 15: Grjotagja Cave

This cave is also a previously hidden gem in North Iceland that became famous after the shooting of the popular HBO series Game of Thrones. It is a Geothermal hot spring in the Lake Myvatn area. The cave is small, made by a fissure in the crust, and the pool is filled with geothermally heated water. The cave's depth is between a few centimeters to a few meters.

The known history of the cave state was in the 18th century when Jon Markusson, the outlaw, lived there. Before, it was a famous bathing area until the volcanic eruption in Krafla around 1975-1984, which led to the rise in the water's temperature. Though the water is cooling down now, the temperature is still between 40°C to 50°C and can fluctuate at times.

Note: Bathing in the cave is prohibited. And beware of the roof as it is not stable, and the cave was even discovered some of the ceiling's parts fell off.

How to reach the Grjotagja Cave

There is no public transport to the cave, so you will need a private car, and the road is gravel. From Reykjahlid, follow road one towards the East. After a 1km drive, take the exit to the gravel road 860; there, you will see a clear indication of Grjotagja. The place is accessible, and you will see ample parking space in front.

Helpful tips for visiting Grjotagja Cave

●The cave has two entrances, requiring you to climb down a small wall of big rocks. Though it is not difficult, it is not recommended if you have a knee problem.

●The roof is not stable, so be careful

●Bathing in the cave is not allowed

●Remember to take the path above the cave to admire the fissure in the crust.

●No amenities

●It is now a popular place, so it's best to visit early or later in the day.

●Be respectful

●Be careful, especially in winter, because the paths can be slippery.

The Grjotagja Cave entrance

The entrance is filled with rocks that fell off; three people can fit at the bottom of the opening, so if you go there in groups, you must wait, depending on the number of people. While entering, you must climb down into the cave.

The inside of the cave

Inside the cave is a beautiful appearance of deep blue and transparent water with steam hitting your face. Though the temperature rose during the volcanic eruption, it's now at a bearable level. Be Careful and avoid any seismic activity inside the cave, as it can trigger a temperature rise in the water and burn you.

The Grjotagja rift-Lava crust fissure

Above the Grjotagja Cave is a lava crust fissure that is beautiful.

Day 16: Bruggsmidjan Kaldi Brewery

The Bruggsmidjan Kaldi Brewery is an excellent place to have the best beer experience. They have a fantastic brewery technique and serve high-quality beer. You can start and finish your day there. You can also learn about their brewery knowledge and get information about excellent beers to try— the place is Located at Oeldugata 22 Oldugata 22, 621, Dalvik Northeast Region. Contact them via +354 466 2505 or visit their website at https://www.bruggsmidjan.is

Day 17: Grettislaug

Grettislaug originated from one of Iceland's sagas, the Grettis Saga. The story follows the life of Grettir, a big man who lived in North Iceland as an outlaw for twenty years. He has visited many places, and each location has his name attached to them. By law, any person declared an outlaw could be killed without punishment. So imagine how he survives those harsh cold winter months, trying to escape frequent assassination attempts. However, Grettir is a strong man, as we see in the stories associated with the Grettislaug pool. He lived in Drangey, the fortress-like northern island. Famous tales also say he swam from the Drangey shores, 7½ kilometers to the hot spring. He bathed in one of them to prevent the chill of the sea from killing him, and since then, the pool has been named after him.

●The History of the Grettislaug

The Grettislaug is located close to Reykjalaug, another pool used for washing. But, due to Iceland's volatile climate, which constantly changes the country over time, the two pools were lost in the early 20th century. However, since the place has a great history, in 1992, the locals decided to rebuild the site and even added a second pool there. The pool didn't retain its previous name. Instead, it was named after Jon Eriksson, a local who tours Drangey Island and even earned the nickname **'the jarl of Drangey'**; thus, the pool is now called Jar's pool.

●Visiting the Grettislaug Pool

Situated in North Iceland on Skagafjödur shore, the pool has fantastic views of the mountains surrounding it, including

Drangey Island. However, you have to pay before accessing the pool, as it's on private property. The water is around 39°C (102°F), and you will find changing equipment on the site.

Day 18: Transportation Museum at Ystafell

The Transportation Museum at Ystafell is the oldest in Iceland. It's a must-go destination for all car lovers, established in 1998 and opened in July 2000. You will see different transportation modes utilized back then and many pictures of cars, working models, tractors, etc. You will find the most refined car collections and other car accessories.

●The museum's details
It's located in Húsavík, Ystafell 3, Húsavík 64, Iceland. It's open every day from 11 am to 6 pm. The recommended duration is 2.5 hours. You can contact them at +354 861 1213.

Day 19: Askja

Iceland has countless beautiful spots that you can easily access from the Ring Road, which has circles all over the country, leaving most of the country's central region untouched. Askja Caldera is a famous island in the Dyngjufjoll Mountains situated on the Vatnajökull National Park Northern side.

This famous island is around 50sq km and was made by emptying a lava chamber under the earth's surface in a volcanic eruption which led to the roof's collapse. The destination is considered an example of a subsidence cauldron in Iceland, as it contains three interlinked cauldrons. Here, you will see the Öskjuvatn Lake, which has 11 square kilometers and is considered the deepest lake in Iceland, having a depth of 217 meters. The Viti Volcano has a 60m deep geothermal lake containing bright blue water at 22°C. Think of it as a surreal, natural blue lagoon inside a volcano. Seeing this landscape should be among the things you will do on your trip to North Iceland.

Driving to Askja

To reach Askja, you will need a 4×4 vehicle. Don't use a small car because you need good clearance crossing the two rivers. The most straightforward road to reach Askja is the Ring Road or Route 1, passing Akureyri and Myvatn and getting off on Road 901. From Road 901, turn right and follow the F905; from there, you will start experiencing the actual driving adventure. After driving for like 21 km, take road F910 to the end, which is an additional 62 km. You will see the first river crossing 5km after you enter F910. And a few minutes later, you will encounter the second river.

The total river crossing you will meet on the route is trees. You didn't see the first one because it's shallow, so you won't see it as a river crossing on the maps. Beware of the roads, as there are a few road forks and F roads on the route. Also, note that you will meet geo bridges with bridges. If they are closed, don't be scared; get down, open it, cross the bridge and close it back the way you see it. Once you reach the shelter, it's best to get off and ask the ranger or any of the shelter staff about the current condition at Viti and its surroundings. After getting the necessary information, drive along F894 for 20 minutes until you reach a parking area at the road end. This point is the beginning of your hike to Viti.

Also, it will be best if you avoid taking the F88 road, which will be presented as an option to reach Askja on your map. The reason is that the road has a lot of fords and river crossings that are not easy to pass with a 4×4 vehicle. Before giving the route, you will need a special car with enough clearance and a snorkel. So the best thing to do is to stick to the easiest F905/F910 way.

●Hiking the Viti and Öskjuvatn Lake

If you follow the flat volcanic valley, the hike to Viti will take only 45 minutes in every way. Because the area is composed of volcanoes, it was used during the Apollo program training in the 60s to prepare astronauts for lunar missions. You can see the dark expanse changing to different brown shades. Depending on the time you visit the place, you will notice how snow covers the hiking areas, even in summer. Take your time to hike; although the stroll is easy, due to the snow, it can become challenging, especially if you are not wearing the right shoes or boots. Watch your steps because, at times, ice melts, so your feet can step on a block of thin ice filled with water underneath. However, rest assured, the water is a few inches high so that it won't pose any threat; it's just that it doesn't feel comfortable when entering your shoes.

When you reach the Lake Öskjuvatn rim, the first thing that will welcome you is the outstanding views of Iceland. If the climate is good, you will see the reflection of the Dyngjufjoll Mountains perfectly on the Lake. You will see the Crater in the foreground to your right m the name Viti as said earlier, means **'hell.'**

From what the rangers have told you earlier, you will know whether you can go down the Crater and bathe in its waters.

●Bath in Viti

You can only bathe in the Viti if the rangers permit you. That's why it's essential to stop at the shelter we said earlier and know the place's current conditions. The rangers are closer to the Crater so that they will know the best conditions of the area. The steep slope goes down when there is too much rain, and the Crater becomes muddy. Though you can descend, it's still challenging to hike up in the mud due to the steepness and slipperiness. If you aren't permitted to access the place, you will see a wooden 'X' sign on the trail that will take you to the Crater, indicating restricted access.

If, fortunately, you arrive and the trail is in good condition, you can head down the Crater and appreciate the beautiful scenery. Though you can bathe in the Crater, the water is cold, with a temperature of around 22°C. But there is a positive side to it; you can have the geothermal lake in the Volcanic Crater all to yourself. Askja has located in a remote area, so not many people visit the place; there is a possibility that you might be the only one there, so you can enjoy yourself for a while. Note: it lacks lifeguards, so be careful when bathing in the lake. Stay around the shore where you can be reached easily.

●The perfect time to visit

The place is accessible mainly from May to September. The F roads sometimes open later or close early, depending on the climate and road conditions. It's best to check the road.is to know whether the road is open or closed and its conditions entirely. Most times, you can't predict Iceland's weather; it can change quickly and often. If the weather condition is severe, it's best not to go to Askja because driving there can be dangerous, and hiking also can be hazardous. But since it's open in summer, you can visit there any time. If you go there in the evening, there is a high chance you will encounter a beautiful moon rising from the East while the sun sets in the west. Coupled with the volcanic landscape, that makes it a surreal experience.

Day 20: Hörgárdalur and Oxnadalur valley

The valley is an utterly stunning mountain that looks like something from a fairy tale. It's a cathedral-like mountain that you will definitely admire whenever you visit it and will leave a deep impression that will make you want to revisit the place beneath the mountain bis the farm Hraun which was named after Hraundrangi.

The farm is believed to be the birthplace of Iceland poet and scientist Jonas Hallgrímsson, born in 1807 at Öxnadalur and died in 1845. The poet wrote some famous Icelandic poems, so he's beloved by them all. Jónas's grave is at the Pingvellir National Park in South Iceland, one of the only two graves in the national park.

You will see a beautiful grove on the main road in Öxnadalur valley, the Jónas Memorial Grove, consecrated in 1996 and dedicated to his memory. That year was Jonas's 150th anniversary, so the Grove was consecrated in his memory. Inside the Grove is a view dial erected in 1958 by Ferdafélag Íslands, Akureyrardeild. The view dial was the 8th erected in the country, and it describes the height and the names of the mountains surrounding the place. The trees around the site have grown tall to the extent they are blocking the view of the area.

Chapter 4

Awesome areas to have fun from Day 21 to day 30

Day 21: Mt. Hraundrangi

The meaning of the name Hraundrangi is Lava Pillar or Lava Spire. Mt. Drag Fjall divided the two valleys into the öxnadalur and Hörgárdalur. The height of the mountain is up to 1,075 meters and was believed to be unscalable. But in 1956, three people were able to climb the mountain; they were two Icelanders from the Icelandic Air Ground Rescue team and one Lieutenant from the US Air force. It took them almost 60 minutes to climb to the mountain's peak; they said the surface of the mountain's peak held treasure, but that was unfounded. Since then, many people have been climbing the mountain; in 1991, 11 people were able to mount the place, and the number increased to 150 later, and people could rise to the peak of the mountain.

A famous tale about the mountain was that there was a keg in the mountain filled with money; the first person that reached the peak of the hill would get the keg. But, the first known climbers didn't find any trace of the keg, so maybe someone had gone before them and picked it up. Another folklore about the mountain was that the hero of the Icelandic saga, Grettir Ásmundarson climbed the mountain and even left his knife and belt.

The mountain usually appears beautiful and has reached the extent that cars will park to admire it. Driving a little further, you will find yourself in a photography paradise where you can snap beautiful pictures and keep memories. Another way you can see the mountain is by driving behind Hörgárdalur valley; you will see it from the other side of the mountains.

Day 22: Jökulsárgljúfur

The park is another attractive location to visit in North Iceland. It's known for its unique features, such as canyons, waterfalls, and rivers. It was established in 1973, and you can visit it all year round to hike and sightsee.

The Jökulsárgljúfur National Park location

The park is part of the Vatnajökull National Park (which we will discuss later in this book.) The park was named after the Jökulsárgljúfur canyon, which is among the deepest canyons in the whole country. It stretches to 25 km with a width of 500 meters and a depth of 100-120 meters. You will experience multiple breathtaking views along with a great ecosystem. The Jökulsárgljúfur National Park formed the western region of the river, meaning the park is a glacial river canyon. It comprises the northwest area of Vatnajökull National Park and covers over 150 square kilometers of land.

How can you reach the Jökulsárgljúfur National Park

The easiest way to get to this park is by taking a cab. Follow road 85 from Húsavík and reach the Asbyrgi visitor center. The park is a distance of 130km from Akureyri. To get to the canyon, follow route 862 or route 864. But because of the bad weather in Iceland, the roads are closed, so always check the road conditions before following any paths.

Things you can see in the Jökulsárgljúfur National Park.

The Jökulsárgljúfur contains three big waterfalls, craters, and canyons. And the most extensive area in the park includes several trails that can lure hikers. Experienced and novice hikers flock to the site and hike on various tracks. You can call the whole place a photography paradise with a unique scenic view.

The Asbyrgi Canyon looks like a horseshoe shape. The cliffs are up to 100 meters; the gorge is around 1 kilometer wide. The Eyan is the photogenic destination in Asbyrgi.

The Jökulsárgljúfur myths

What makes every spot in Iceland more mesmerizing is the myth associated with it. And the Jökulsárgljúfur National Park is no exception. In the folklore related to Asbyrgi, the locals believed that the hoof print of Sleipnir, Odin's eight-legged horse, the Vikings that settled there early. And the U shape was formed after the horse's hooves crashed onto the surface. It's also believed that elves can be seen mid-night dancing near Botnstjorn Pond.

●The formation of the Jökulsárgljúfur National Park

The canyon was formed thousands of years ago after the glacial burst. The event happened 10,000 years ago and occurred 3,000 years ago, also. The glacial floods carved most landforms, such as the deep gorge, ravines, and basins. The park was formed in 1973.

●Things you can see in the Jökulsárgljúfur National Park

As we said in the beginning, the Jökulsárgljúfur National Park has a lot of scenic destinations you can see and even snap pictures such as Dettifos, Selfoss, and Hafragilsfoss.

●Hiking at Jökulsárgljúfur

Hiking the Jökulsárgljúfur is really rewarding. You will see marked trails at the edge of the canyon cater to help you. So check and know which one you can handle before trying it. The four areas within the park own popular hiking routes; the Asbyrgi, Vesturdalur, Dettifoss, and Holmatungur. All the trails contain abbreviations to help you. Even though you don't need to hike before appreciating the park's beauty, you can pick any of the famous trails.

●Accommodations near the Jökulsárgljúfur National Park

Near the Jökulsárgljúfur National Park is Húsavík city. You can lodge there in any of their hotels.

●Camp in the Jökulsárgljúfur National Park

You can find a lot of camping grounds in Asbyrgi and Dettifoss. There is also one close to Vesturdalur. You will find necessary facilities on the camping ground like electricity, toilets, cooking areas, washing machines, etc.

Things you should know before visiting Jökulsárgljúfur National Park

●From the park, you can see Asbyrgi.

●The park is not accessible in winter, so the best time to visit is in summer.

●There is no sunset in the last two weeks of June.

●The park will surely change your perspective on the powers of nature.

Day 23: Pinkgekirkja church

For people that love history, visiting the Pingeykirkja church should be one of the things you should do on your trip to North Iceland. The Pingeykirkja is considered among the most beautiful Churches in Iceland. Located at Pinggeyrar, it's isolated by Húnafjördur bay. The church was consecrated in 1877 and is among the few stone churches in Iceland. The stone in Pinkgeykirkja was found in the Ásbjarnarnesbjörd, 8 kilometers away from the church. The walls inside the church are one meter thick, and it's so beautiful. The church is popularly known for its ceiling, which is blue and painted with 1000 golden stars. Some windowpanes match the stars on the roof.

Most people that visit the church to see the stars on the ceiling are in awe when they see other stunning artifacts in the church.

●An altarpiece in the Pingeykirkja

The altarpiece in the church is the oldest one, dating back to the 14th century. The piece is the only artifact left in Pingeykirkja from the Catholic period. The pulpit was donated to the church by Lauritz Gottrup in 1696 from the Netherlands. And aside from the pulpit, he donated multiple other artifacts to the church.

The first monastery in Pinggeyrar, Iceland, was erected in 1133, and it remained until 1550 during the reformation of the place. The sanctuary is famously known for its literature, written from 1100 to 1300 on parchment.

●Inside the Pingeykirkja

An archaeological dig inside the church in the summer of 2018 dates back to the sedimentary strata from the 17th and 18th centuries. The archaeologist found a structure erected at the church's peak that looked like it had been more extensive than the current stone church. The system they found was believed to be used for human habitation. There is also a fine chalk pipe carved with a head of a man found in a refuse dump.

Jón Ögmundsson, the Bishop of Hólar, pledged to erect a church and a manor in the place if they would stop famine in the country. And when they stopped the famine, the Bishop fulfilled his promise. One of the most extensive manors in Iceland was also erected in a pinger which is a resident of the chieftains. So the history of this place is quite fascinating. The name Pingeyrar was derived from the word Ping, which means parliament, and it was named this due to the assemblies held in the place in Húnaping from 930 to 1264, during the Commonwealth period.

At the church, you will see a visitor center titled Klausturstofa. The center was built because of the Pingeykirkja church, thanks to the stone and the church's compliments. You will pay a small fee from the visitor center and be guided to the Church.

The Vatnsdæla saga took place in the Vatnsdalur valley. And the tale was written in the monastery at Pingeyrar in 1270. It tells the history of the people that lived in this part of the country.

●Klausturstofa

On the visitor's center walls, you will see drawings from the saga in the Vatnsdalur valley. You will also see a replica of the Flateyjarbók, the Flatey Book, the most prominent manuscript written from 1387 to 1394 that dates back to the middle ages. It consists of the history of the Norwegian kings.

●Opening times

The Pingeykirkja church visitor center is usually open in summer from June 1st to August 31st from 10 am to 5 pm. Many people drive and pass the place without knowing it is another beautiful tourist attraction center.

How to reach the church

If you are coming from Reykjavik, follow North on ring road one, turn left to road 721, and drive for about 6 kilometers. You will find it midway between the Blönduós and Hvammstangi towns, and you can even view it on the road from a distance.

Day 24: Brunir Horse

The brunir horse is run by a family living in Eyjafjördur, North Iceland. The family has made the farm a tourist attraction center where you can see the brunir horse. The main attractive event of the place is the horse show. The family organized professional horse shows where the horses were introduced in their natural form, history, uniqueness, skills, and diversity.

The company also has a studio and an exhibition area where

you can watch paintings made by the farmers for sale. You will also see other artworks created by some famous artists. You can also eat local cuisine the family serves in their small Café. You can eat soups, salads, light courses, desserts, and coffee. And the food is made with fresh ingredients from the area.

When traveling to Eyjafjordur, you can make a stop and brunir horse, learn about the unique Icelandic horses, and even get information about the farmer's daily life. So once you are finished exploring the farm and its surroundings, you can order a hearty launch, sit and enjoy your sumptuous meal.

Day 25: Hverir

Hverir is one of the top attractive sites in North Iceland. The place is also known as Námafjall, Námasjard, or Hverarönd. It's a unique destination on the diamond circle and among the best attractions at Lake Myvatn. Like most of the areas in Iceland, Hverir is also a volcanic origin-destination. It's a Geothermal Area under the Námafjall mountain and belongs to the Krafla Volcano fissure zone. It has a depth of 1000 meters, and the temperature is above 200°C. The water flowing below the surface gets heated quickly and returns to the surface after changing to steam. The fumarole gas has hydrogen sulfide, which causes rotten egg smell characteristics that increase the place's attractiveness and make it a site where everyone wants to have fun. Get ready to experience bubbling mud pools, hissing fumaroles, and colorful ground cracks. You can access the place easily from Ring road, so whenever you are passing along the road, do your best to stop and try this unique destination.

●Why you should visit the Hverir Geothermal Area

This geothermal area is worth visiting and is absolutely surreal. The grounds in Hverir are rich in minerals coupled with bubbles and smoke. From overlooking the barren land from the viewing platforms, you will observe that NASA used the place as a training ground for astronauts. This reason also makes it a must-visit area in North Iceland.

Visit the Hverir Geothermal Area

Before you even reach the geothermal area, it will reveal itself from a distance. The road from Dettifoss to Lake Myvatn is flat and has several curves. You will see steam emerging from the vents at a distance. You will perceive the rotten egg smell that most people hate when the wind blows you. But don't worry; as you get close to the colorful ground, you will be welcome by steam vents, mud pools, and fumaroles. Despite its unpleasant first impression, you will receive pure joy in the place. Right from where you park your car, you will begin your adventure. You will read information about the area, which is a good introduction; you will receive a glimpse of what the site contains, and you will perceive a strong smell of hydrogen sulfide that will attack your senses through your nose. You will later adjust to the odor after some minutes. If you want, you snap some pictures of the area, then move to the bubble mud pools, hissing vents, steaming fumaroles, earth cracks, and the ground, colored by minerals. You will also see a trail that will guide you to visit all the beautiful attractions of the area, so you don't have to worry about getting lost or missing the road. On those windy days, the steam usually changes direction after every minute, and the whole place will give a different appearance. Note: make sure to be on the designated trail all the time because all the elements there can be harmful.

The Namafjall Hike

Your visit to Hverir is incomplete if you didn't hike Namafjall mountain. It's relatively easy; within one hour, you can round the whole area and view it from a different perspective, and the place is less crowded. The appearance of the other sceneries is even better when you view it from above. You will also get a bonus view of the other side of the area from a distance of

Myvatn Lake.

The trail head

Hiking to Namafjall begins at Hverir, so the trails start from either the northwest or the southwest part of the place. Standing on the main viewing platform at the parking space, you will see the routes leading to the mountain from both the right and left sides.

Clockwise or anticlockwise?

Even though Namafjall Hike is a loop, you can follow any side you want. Most people begin their hike from the right side due to the lower steepness of the place. But as we said, you can follow it from whichever side you like.

The trail

The first few minutes on the trail are steeper. You will be elevated at around 100 meters. The other part of the trail is passable. The views from the trail are much better and more visible.

The time you will spend in the area

Well, you might need a lot of time, and sometimes you can tour the place quickly. It all depends on the weather condition and your preference. If the weather is convenient, you can do everything slowly and appreciate the breathtaking view of the place. Thirty minutes is sufficient for you to do everything if the weather condition is pleasant, and if it isn't, you can round things up within 15 or 20 minutes. This time is just for you to tour the place; if you are going to hike, add like 1hour to the time we mentioned above.

How to reach the Hverir Geothermal Area

The main entrance to Hverir is off the ring road. You can access the road from your left side by traveling the road clockwise.

●Going by car

Visiting Hverir by far is the best convenient way to reach the place. You can freely roam around and visit the top attractions in Iceland at your own pace. You can also visit other destinations along the way. You don't need to have a 4WD car to visit Hverir, especially in summer, because the road is perfectly paved at this time. But in winter, it's better to get a 4WD vehicle because the road might be icy or slippery.

●Using public transport

There is no public transport that goes to Hverir directly, so whenever you stop one, ask them whether they are willing to drop you there or not. And note that the Public transport that goes around the area works only once daily. So when you reach there, you must look for a means to come back anyway. Amazingly, you don't need to pay any fees to enter Hverir, and it's open 24/7, so get ready, find a good car or public transport that can drop you off the road, and you are good to go.

Places you can stay near Hverir

Hverir is near Lake Myvatn, so you can just lodge there. Or you can stay in any of these hotels, Sel-Hotel Myvatn, Fosshótel Húsavík, Lake Hotel Egilsstadir, Akureyri Hostel, etc.

Day 26: Aldeyjarfoss

Iceland is filled with multiple beautiful natures and wildlife, including the Aldeyjarfoss, considered one of the most beautiful waterfalls in the country. It's situated in the Northern Highlands in Budardalur valley. It passes through a narrow canyon and is covered by twisted basalt columns where you can appreciate the perfect view of the powerful landscape. Some Icelanders consider this place a hidden gem; once you discover it, you will understand why they do so, especially with its countless treasures. And although it's not easily accessible, once you visit there, you will know it is worth the visit. The waterfall's backdrop is a black basalt rock cliff, and exactly at its center is a falls drop that creates a stellar display of different colors. Aldeyjarfoss is not that high, just 20 meters, but it will give you the same impression you got from the taller cascades in the country. The falls originate in the largest glacier in Europe, Vatnajökull, and the water flowing is called the Skálfandsfljót river (the river that feeds the Godafoss waterfall.)

Amazing facts about Aldeyjarfoss
- The waterfall is said to resemble Svartifoss in Skaftafell.
- You can drive to the top of the waterfall
- Glacier in Europe feeds the waterfall
- The waterfall is mainly considered the best photography point in the whole of Iceland
- You can't find restrooms in the parking space.

Aldeyjarfoss waterfall location
The waterfall is situated in North Iceland, at the end of the mountain road Sprengisandur. It's 75 kilometers from

Akureyri and 40 kilometers from Godafoss waterfall.

How to reach the waterfall

Reaching Aldeyjarfoss waterfall can be a little tricky. For example, you must first ensure that your rental car has access to F-roads. Secondly, you must check the weather condition of the place before you visit it. Thirdly you have to reach the area when there is still light; you can't go there at night because the waterfall is situated in an isolated place where you can't find any city nearby or street light to help you. The drive from Akureyri to the waterfall usually takes 1 hour and 15 minutes. Take the ring road route one and follow the eastern direction; make a right turn onto road 842. Keep driving on this road, then make a turn and follow road F26 which will take you near the waterfall. Once you park in the parking space, reaching the waterfall takes only 10 minutes. Take the narrow way along the Skjálfandafjót River, and beautiful black basalt columns and the wonders of the Aldeyjarfoss waterfall will welcome you. Note: in summer, you can use any car for the drip, but in winter, it's best to use a 4×4 vehicle.

Dining areas near Aldeyjarfoss

It's impossible to find dining areas near Aldeyjarfoss waterfall; the nearest you can get is Akureyri or other tourist attractions near the waterfall, such as the Reykjahid, Myvatn, and Godafoss. The closest restaurant is about 50 kilometers from the waterfall, so you should have your lunch while going there and have a mini picnic. And upon returning, take everything with you, don't throw cabbage anyhow; you will even find a trashcan in the parking space. Visit the place, maintain its hygiene, and leave it untouched.

Accommodations near the Aldeyjarfoss waterfall

You can lodge in nearby hotels such as the Laxá hotel, hotel Myvatn, and hótel Edda Stórutjarnir. Guesthouses, B&B's, Farmstays such as Kidagil Guesthouse, Sandhaugar Guesthouse, Strong, Fosshóll, Fljótsbakki farm, or Skútustadir Farmer's guesthouse.

Camping grounds near Aldeyjarfoss waterfall

The best camping ground near Aldeyjarfoss waterfall is the Camping Harmar. It has all the facilities you will need, such as bathrooms, changing sites, showers, washing machines, cooking equipment, an indoor sleeping lodge, electricity, WiFi, a playground, boat rental, and walking paths. It's open year-round, and adults pay around 1600 ISK per night.

The Waterfall in winter

You can visit the waterfall there, but the road can be dangerous and difficult to pass in winter. So the best way to avoid such circumstances is to check the weather before your visit. Here, it doesn't mean you should check the weather a week earlier; instead, you should check it close to the journey because Iceland's weather can change abruptly.

Day 27: Goesea Spa

The Geosea Geothermal Sea Baths are considered the most beautiful in the world. They are three unique pools that cling to the cliffs from above Skjálfandi bay. Below the ocean are a few whales and dolphins. By sitting on the hot water and directly facing the snow-capped Kinnarfjöll mountains from a distance, you will have a perfect view of the country: Iceland, fire, and ice. Among the geothermal baths in Iceland, the Geosea is the best, composed of salt water and unparalleled beauty.

Another thing that makes these baths the best ones is the location and the design. Also, no matter the time you visit the pool, be it summer or winter, you will really enjoy it. You will undoubtedly see why Time magazine mentioned it among the 100 most beautiful places on earth.

How to visit the Geosea baths

The architectural firm that designed the Blue Lagoon near Reykjavik was the one that designed the Geosea baths. And now it's more famous than the Blue Lagoon. The place was designated to blend into the mountain without disrupting the ocean view. The entrance will take you to the ground where the pools are situated. Polished black lava rocks and stale gray stones were used to make the place and the pools, making the whole structure look like it has disappeared into the mountains.

Once you arrive, you will pay the entrance fee and receive an electronic bracelet to wear while you are there. If you have visited other Icelandic hot springs like the Blue Lagoon, the bracelet is similar to that of the one they gave you there. The bracelet is the ticket to enter the Geosea spa area, it will open and close your locker, and you can use it to charge drinks at the swim-up bar. After you pay the entrance fee, use your bracelet and pass through the turnstile, remove your shoes, and leave them in the shoe racks. The locker rooms are separated by gender. Once there, you can arrange your things inside the locker and take your bathing suit to the shower. Iceland generally has a particular bathing rule for hot springs and spas. You can only wear your bathing suit after taking a shower completely naked and washing your hair, feet, and private parts. When leaving the hot springs, you will pay your bar tab and leave. Using your wristband, swipe out and exit the turnstile. If this is the first time you use the wristband and are confused about it, you can ask any of the locals or the helpful staff questions.

●The infinity pools

Geosea features three different hot springs pools. The upper pool is Located in the corner of the building, and the temperature there is in the middle of the three. The pool also contains a swim-up window where you can order drinks like beer, wine, a sofa, and juice. The glass will be charged to your wristband, which you will pay when leaving. Water is free there.

The pool you see immediately outside is the hottest one, far away from the yellow lights house. The hot water comes from it and supplies the other pools; there is also a steam room nearby. The most excellent pool is the largest and most famous among the three. It has a circular design, and you can view the whole of Skjálfandi bay from its edge.

The water at Geosea pools circulates every three hours, so you don't have to worry about getting cold or dirty. It also flows through the pools frequently at a rate of 20L per second, meaning the saltwater doesn't need to be treated with chemicals.

The water in the Geosea baths is from a borehole drilled while looking for hot water for geothermal energy. The drill was unsuccessful; it broke through a fissure filled with hot seawater that was too corrosive and had abundant minerals to heat houses around the area. The locals make the place a seawater bathing pool. So the water in the Geosea pools is from the two drill holes. The pools were open to visitors in 2018.

●Things you should carry when going to the Geosea baths

To make your visit more enjoyable, you will need to carry certain things such as a bathing suit because it's required to take it to the pools, a towel which you will need after showering, the robe which is helpful to wear between the locker room and the pools, water shoes because the place is artificial. Hence, the bottom is smooth; the boots protect you from stubbing your toe or hitting a rock, and biodegradable sunscreen, especially in summer, protects you from sunburn.

How to reach the Geosea baths

The pool is situated on the sea cliffs above Húsavík and Skjálfandi bay. From the ring road, it will take 35 to 45 minutes to get there. If you are coming from Akureyri, follow route 1 through the Vadla Heidi tunnels. From the other side of the tunnel, follow the defined high that heads north-highway 85 in the Húsavík direction.

After reaching the town, you will pass a big church on your right and a harbor on your left. Pass the dock and find the second road that heads uphill to the left. Once you reach there, follow the Geosea signs, it will take you uphill, where you will follow right to Höfdavegur. On your left, look for a big yellow house. Be careful while using GPS and mobile phone apps because they can give you wrong directions that will take you to the harbor instead of the Geosea baths.

●Opening days

The hot spring is always open, even on Christmas day. In summer, from 1st May to 1st September, the pool is available from early morning to late at night. The time is reduced during winter, generally from 12 pm to 10 pm. The opening time can change abruptly due to the unstable weather in the country. So it's best to consult the pool's website to know the current opening hours.

●Price

Geosea pools are less expensive than the famous Blue Lagoon and Myvatn Nature Baths. The cost is usually 4500 ISK for adults and 2000 ISK for children.

●Accommodations near the Geosea baths

Though you can visit the baths and do everything within a day, staying overnight is better if you want to enjoy the Geosea and watch whales. You can lodge in any of these hotels. The Fosshotel Húsavík is just a 19-minute walk from Geosea, the Barnabas Apartments is a 17-minute walk from Geosea, and the Húsavík Cape Hótel, which is a 10-minute walk from the Geosea baths.

●Dining centers in Geosea baths

Though there is a small Café in the area, what they offer is qualitative but limited. You can find soup sandwiches and snacks. If you want to eat something more substantial, you can visit other dining centers in Húsavík, such as the Salka restaurant, the most popular dining area in the town, and the

Naustid restaurant, run by a small family, where you can find a lot of Icelandic cuisine including seafood.

Day 28: Hvitserkur sea stack

The Hvítserkur is popularly known as the troll of northwest Iceland. The place is stunning and worth visiting. The majestic Hvítserkur stands majestically 50 meters offshore. It resembles an animal, more like an elephant, a rhino, or a dinosaur drinking. When you visit in summer, you will see many Fulmer nesting on the sea sack making the whole place look alive. The name Hvítserkur means Hvit means white, and Serkur means a long shirt. The folklore behind this place is that the Hvítserkur is a petrified troll that lived in Standir in Westford's and wanted to tear the bells at the Pingeyraklaustur convent. The trolls aren't following Christianity, so they hate the sound and sight of a church or bells. The trolls are fortunately caught by sunlight and turn into stone by daylight.

Hvítserkur is a volcanic dyke that was eroded by the sea. It was in danger of sea eruption, so the base had to be strengthened with concrete. The place was ruined in 1955 to the extent the locals had to start a collection to save the dyke.

From another angle, you will see the view of the Hvítserkur looking white and different. The road to the place is a gravel one from Oscar hostels that will directly take you to the parking space, where you will see benches and tables. You can see this beautiful dyke from above or just walk to it. From the parking space, a trail will take you near it and view it from above. You will see a steep trail from there that will take you to the beach. You can also go to the beach directly from the parking space. However, in the summertime, you can reach Hvítserkur because of the cranky Arctic tern. So prepare a stick or umbrella to chase them away when they attack you. Sometimes, they are persistent and don't give up quickly, so you might be the one to retreat.

Among the tourist attraction in the area is one of the largest seal colonies in Iceland. You will find many seals resting on the beach. The shore is covered in a giant multicolored jellyfish that makes it attractive and unique; the jellyfish come in blue and golden coloration. And this is the only place you will see so many of these beautiful creatures in one place.

Near the Hvítserkur is another worth-visiting site, the Ánastadastapi rock. And just like Hvítserkur, you can't visibly see the Ánastadastapi rock from the road. To visit the rock, follow the steep down the grassy hill, which will take you to the monolith. The stone is more colorful compared to the Hvítserkur. And slight Hvítserkur resembles a dinosaur; the Ánastadaspi rock is just a monolith.

Walking a little further, you will be greeted with a white and green painted sheep roundup, the Hamarsrétt roundup. The roundup is available in many places all over the country. In summer, Icelandic sheep can roam around freely and gather in September. The roundups then separate the sheep, and this is what makes the place so unique.

Day 29: Arctic Henge

The Arctic Henge is located in a small town on the North East side of Iceland. It consists of a 46-meter tall gate and a 110-meter high column. The gate work as a sundial because they capture sunlight and casts shadows on the place. The henge was inspired by the four cardinal dwarves from Norse Mythology, Austria, Nordri, Sudri, and Vestri, which are now East, North-South, and West. You will find the history of the four dwarves in the Prose Edda Book. Each is assigned a role by Odin, who Icelanders consider the God of wisdom.

The dwarves here are also assigned another role along with the 68 dwarves mentioned in the Völuspá, which all together form a calendar. The dwarves, both all and new, with their peculiar names, aligned together and create a chronological circle. The circle is based on terms related to the four seasons. And up till today, what leads to mentioning the 68 dwarves in Völuspa is still a mystery, even though their names are related to the year's structure. Aside from this exciting history, lighting near the Arctic henge ghost is a natural phenomenon.

The Arctic henge is set in Raufarhöfn, among the country's remote and northernmost towns. The henge is still under construction, just like its ancient predecessor, Stonehenge. The purpose of the henge is to capture sunlight, cast its shadows in a specific location, and capture the light between the aligned gateways.

The history of the Arctic Henge

The idea of this arctic henge came from the innovator Erlingur Thoroddsen's speculation that there is a possible way to use the endless expanse since there is nothing on the horizon and the midnight sun. They also propose an idea to use the dwarf's names from Völuspa and customize some parts of the sagas. Artists Haukur Halldórsson and Erlingur worked together on the pictures and even made sketches and models that helped in the work.

Nobody can explain the dwarves in Völuspa aside from the Austri, Vestri, Nordri, and the Sudri, which are the East, West, North, and South. If you connect the dwarves' names with the annual season, it's possible to connect them to the yearly circle of 72 weeks—the dwarves were believed to be some almanac with each dwarf controlling five days. The dwarves were given roles based on their personalities. The dwarves can be connected to birthdays, and people can link to their dwarves.

Inside the henge are the 68 dwarves standing around a circular trail. Inside the henge is also a polar star pointer. You will also see the home of the sun, which is meant to be where visitors will sit down and take pictures. There is a hall ray between the high columns and a seat where visitors can empty their minds and replenish their energy. You will also find an altar of fire and water which will remind you of the power of the elements; you can perform events like weddings and oath-taking in the place.

How to reach the Arctic Henge

From Húsavík, the distance to the place is about 130 kilometers, so it will take you around 1.5 hours to reach on a good road. Take road 85 northwest of Húsavík, pass Asbyrgi, and take the 874 route junction east before Kópasker. Once you go to Raufarhöfn, you will see the stone standing majestically on the hills above the town. You can find a drive to take you to the henge or walk since it's not far.

Places you can visit near the henge

●Raufarhöfn

You can hike and swim in hot tubs, ice baths, saunas, and a gym. You will even get a dhar fishing tour from an experienced fishing guide in the lakes

●Melkrakkaslétta

This is a plain area where you can fish, watch birds, and enjoy nature, especially in spring and summer.

●Raudinúlpur

You can have a stunning view of birds on the Karl or Kerling rocks.

●Höskuldarnes

This is a newly built bird-watching center near the Hölkus-darnes firm, which you can see from the road.

●Raudales

You can hike in this area which is around 7 kilometers and only 30 mins drive from Raufarhöfn. You can also see different bird species and puffins here.

Day 30: Borgarvirki

Though folktales say the Borgarvirki is an old fortress, there is no evidence to prove their claim. We can at least believe it is small because it's a volcanic plug that looks like an ancient fortress, standing impressive and stunning. From the parking lot, it will take you only four minutes to rule, and it's close to Hvítserkur, so you can kill two birds with one stone, visit Hvítserkur and visit the Borgarvirki simultaneously.

How to visit Borgarvirki

Located in the Vatnsnes peninsula in North Iceland, you can visit it on a relaxed self-drive or follow the 7-day Arctic coast way self-drive accessible in summer.

Chapter 5

Keep unforgettable memories from Day 31 to day 40

Day 31: Drangey Bird Cliff

Visiting the Drangey Bird Cliff will always remain a memorable trip for you. The place is located in the Skagafjödur fjord North Iceland. You can only climb to the cliff following one way, from the Uppgönguvik or climbing up the cove. The path is steep and reaches up to the top of the 180 meters high cliff. The climbing is easy because you will find ropes and chains and a ladder on the final climb.

●**Climb the Drangey Bird Cliff**

The Drangey Bird Cliff is written in most of Iceland's historical books and is among the best-known Vikings in the country. Grettir, the strongest Ásmundarson, also sought refuge in his last year as an outlaw from the Drangey Bird Cliff. He stayed here for three years with his brother Illigu and his slave Glaumur. His brother stays with him because Grettir is afraid of the dark and doesn't want to stay alone in Drangey. And since Drangey has only one way to climb up, Grettir decides to take it as his asylum; moreover, if they remove the ladder, there won't be even a way to climb up, so he's safe in the place.

The current Drangey has ropes and chains to help people climb to the top and a ladder to do the final climb. Though the place is a bit steep, even children can do this tour, and we assure you they will love it.

You will first arrive at a spot titled Gvendaraltari, which is Gvendur altar, named after Gudmundur, the bishop that consecrated the island after the accidents that happened. You will also see a plague rock with Fadirvorid, which means Lord's Prayer in the Icelandic language. And before you ascend further, you are required to say the prayer out loud.

Once you reach the top of the cliff, you can visit the Drangey-jarskáli hut, built in 1984. You will also walk to the area where Grettir built his cabin, the Grettisbæli or Grettir Lair. The northern wind sheltered him in the place, and he collected water from the rocks in small bowls. Seeing the holes Grettir drank water from 10 centuries ago is so awesome.

Grass has covered the tip of the steep rock, and some 80 sheep from the farmers grazed in the area when Grettir was living there. You will also find many birds on the cliff and an abundance of eggs. So the people living there never lacked food. As time goes on, there are all 80 sheep except one called Hösmagi, which they decide not to kill because it entertains them. Possibly, the Hösmagi is the leader among the sheep.

Grettir stayed on the cliff for about three years before he got slain in the place when a witch cast a spell on the log, and it landed on the ridge. Though Grettir wanted to cut the spell as a firework, the magic, unfortunately, broke his axe, and some parts of the axe landed on his foot and caused him a bad injury. The leg swelled and looked dark blue. And while he was wounded, his enemy porbjörn the Viking climbed the cliff and killed him. He used Grettir's sword and killed Illugu and Glaumur.

Grettir was to be hanged because he was believed to have burnt some 12 men alive. Though we can say it's not entirely Grettir's fault following the tale that says he entered a rest house where the 12 men were living asking them for fire, they misunderstood him and thought he was a troll, so they attacked him with firebrands leading to a fire outbreak.

From here, you will hike to the top, around 180 meters high. You can stop at the cliff's edge and see the Grettisbrunna or the Grettir well, where he collected water; you will also find other places named after Grettir.

Once you reach the cliff's top, your guide will take you to the cliff's edge, which looks scary in the fog. The guide will ask you to hold your hands behind your eyes; this way, you will hear the sounds of the birds under the cliffs multiplied. It's interesting to stand on the cliffs and listen to the squawk of the birds, and at every angle, you look at are birds.

The birds on this cliff are one of the things that add beauty to the place. Some bird species you will find include the Guillemot, puffin, auk, etc. You will see plenty of young ravens in the fog and multiple puffins.

The puffin is the most popular bird in the country and is what attracts most of Iceland's visitors. It's pretty spectacular, especially with its multicolored beak. You will find puffins all over these cliffs, and you can snap pictures to keep memories.

Also, there are multiple puffin holes about 3 meters long; you can walk on the tip of the holes and explore the rock's top. Though it might sound strange knowing that you are almost stepping on the puffins, you walk with care so you won't stumble or get your feet stuck in the holes.

In spring, birds are caught in Drangey, and their eggs are collected. For this purpose, you will even see ropes and ladders in multiple places on the island. We can say the people doing this work are brave and aren't afraid of heights. Drangey is often called the pearl of Skagafjödur because it has been a good food source for the people living there and is even a landmark in the fjord.

●The Kerling Rock

On the southern side of Drangey is a steep rock called Kerling (which in the Icelandic language means the old lady) standing alone in the sea. And on the North side, there used to be a rock called Karl (the older man), but an earthquake that happened centuries ago led to Karl's collapse.

You can see these kinds of rocks with similar names in many places in Iceland. The history is that the rocks were trolls caught in the sunlight, which turned into stone by rays of sunlight.

Even Karl and Kerling were believed to be passing the fjord with their cow. Then daylight turned them into stone, and the cow turned into the Drangey cliff. The two stones look pretty fascinating in the fog. We can even say the mist gave the island some mysterious vibe and awesomeness.

Back to the story of Grettir the strong. He had few friends on the mainland when he was alive; his friends lived at the Reykir farm in Reykjaströnd. There was a day their fire got extinguished; Grettir swam for up to seven kilometers to the mainland to get the fire from his friends, and the event was named the Drangeyjarsund swim. He warmed up in the Reykir natural hot pool when he reached ashore. In the Grettir saga, this event was described as how Grettir cooked himself in the hot pool for an aiming period before he visited his friends to receive the fire. Grettislaug, discussed above, is a replica of the hot spring.

●Soak in Jarlslaug

The Jarlslaug, which means 'the pool of Earl,' was built in memory of the late Jón Eriksson Drangeyjarjarl. Jón was Drangeyjarferdir, your operator for plenty of years, and was the one that made the Grettislaug pool. His son and grandson are now the ones operating the Drangeyjarferdir tours.

Drangey Bird Cliff's opening hours

The island is primarily open from 20th May to 20th August, and the hours are usually 3 and ½ hours. To visit there, you can take a boat that operates daily, and the ride takes about 25 minutes.

Day 32: Kolugljufur Canyon and Kolufoss Waterfall

Visiting Iceland is one of the trips that you will never forget. And the remarkable thing is that when you think you have finished visiting all the exciting places, you will discover another wonderful area you have never heard about, and you will feel like you want to start all over again. You will never want to miss multiple hidden gems in the country, including the Kolugljufur Canyon and the Kolufoss waterfall. Amazingly, the canyon is just a short drive from the ring road and among the country's best off-the-beaten paths.

What you should know about the Kolugljufur Canyon and Kolufoss Waterfall

Most of the beginning of every fantastic place in Iceland starts from a river. This is even obvious given the name of the county, Ice and Fire. The Kolufoss Waterfall, previously known as Vididalsa river, is a famous salmon river that makes its way up north. Though this place itself isn't much interesting, the combination of the cascading water flowing into a narrow gorge is the attractive side of the waterfall.

The size of the Kolugljufur Canyon is around 1 kilometer long, 60 meters wide, and 40 meters deep. So you can walk around the canyon as much as you can. Like other natural attractions in the country, the gorge also has a history behind it, telling how it came into existence.

As written in the history books, the canyon became known when a giantess called Kola lived in it. It was said that she hung salmons, cooked them, and her actions resulted in the gorge's shape.

●Trip to the Kolugljufur Canyon

Going to the canyon is pretty easy once you reach its parking space. Though you should be careful while visiting the place in summer because annoying insects fill it, keep your bug repellent or keep moving while driving them away.

●The Kolufoss Waterfall

Once you reach here, you can get out of your car and cross the bridge to view the waterfall fully. After appreciating the view, walk behind the bridge and turn left; you will be greeted with a fantastic viewpoint to snap some photos.

●The Kolugjufur Canyon

When you are done with the waterfall, you can turn your attention to the Kolugljufur Canyon and focus on the gorge. After returning to the bridge, on the right side of the bridge is a small viewing platform. Once you are done with it, you can continue along the gorge. You will find a narrow path that can be slippery when it rains or snows. Be careful while passing there. In addition, the place lacks safe barriers to protect you from falling or slipping. While walking the path, you can admire the high cliffs and the river constantly finding its way through the narrow gorge.

The amount of time you need to complete your trip in the Kolugjufur Canyon

How much time you need depends on what you want to do on the bridge. For example, if you want to snap pictures and go, it will take you only 15 minutes to finish. But if you want to slowly tower the canyon and follow the paths along the gorge for a while, this can take up to 40 or 50 minutes, depending on your pace.

How to reach the Kolugjufur Canyon

From the ring road, it will only take you around 15 minutes to reach the canyon. However, it used to get little traffic now because it's getting more famous.

Rent a car

Rent a car or camper van. Once in the car, take Road 715 until you reach the gorge. And even though it's an unpaved road, it's still in good condition so that you can get to the place even in your 2WD vehicle. The situation can change in winter because snow blocks the road though the locals help plow the routes. So if you plan to visit the place in winter, you should rent a 4WD vehicle and have snow chains.

Use public transport

You won't find public transport that will take you to the canyon; you rent a car or take a tour.

Use a tour

Because the canyon is an off-the-beaten-path area, a few tours have it in their place. You can follow the North Iceland Tour from Reykjavik, which will take you to the best of the wild, including the Kolufoss Waterfall and the Kolugljufur Canyon.

Where to lodge when you visit the area

Well, you might tour the place within a day; if you want a

better view and appreciate the night scenery, you will need to stay the night. And although there are no hotels on the site, you can find a few new places, such as the Vididalstunga, Daeli Guesthouse, the Sigló Hotel, Akureyri Hostel, etc.

Best time to visit the site.
Theoretically, the site is available in all seasons. The place can be open between October to May when snow falls, though the parking space might be blocked. But, in summer, the visit is less challenging since everywhere is almost dry, so summer is the best time to go there.

Day 33: Reykjavik

Reykjavik means Smokey Bay. The city is the Northernmost national capital in the world and has the smallest population compared to any other Capital City. It's home to almost 150,000 residents. It has excellent sights to see, many activities related to culture and nature, and even energetic nightlife.

Things you can do in Reykjavik

As far as a small city, you have multiple reasons to visit the place. For example, despite its size, it's one of the best places you can go to in North Iceland, and also you can explore it on foot, so you don't have to look for a vehicle. Multiple things in Reykjavik can attract your attention, such as its wildlife experience, unique architecture, dining on world-class cuisines, hunting from the street, and many more. In addition, you don't have to worry about language as most people there speak English.

How to reach Reykjavik

Iceland is an Iceland, so means of reaching it are sometimes minimal. The most used method is air; if you are coming on a plane, there is a small airport in Reykjavik. But if you are coming on an international flight from North America or Europe, you will first arrive at the Keflavik International Airport. You can take a bus or taxi and reach the capital, just 32 miles from the airport. You can also follow ferries, though they only operate once a week between April to October, so if you, fortunately, come within these months, you can take a ferry service.

Top things to do in the capital

Reykjavik has several fun activities to welcome you and make your stay the most memorable one.

●The Reykjavik swimming pools

We all know Iceland is defined by water, from its mighty glaciers to the rolling waves of the Atlantic Ocean and the Geothermal Pools. So this should make sense why Reykjavik also has plenty of swimming pools so visitors and Icelanders can take a dip. So what better way to appreciate the beautiful city than joining the locals and visiting one of the pools in Reykjavik? Thanks to the county's policies, water usage in multiple places in Iceland is nearly free. Moreover, going to swimming pools is among the best things you should do, especially if you visit in winter. Most of the pool's water is heated and accessible all year round.

Reykjavik alone has 18 swimming pools, each containing indoor and outdoor pools, a sauna, and at least one hot tub. We can say the pools in this country are more like a luxury spa you find around. The entrance fee for the pools here in Reykjavik is usually about 8 USD. And if you want something more natural, the Geothermal-heated water at Reykjavik beach, Nautholsvik, and Grotta Lighthouse will do the trick. Most of these pools are fabulous and free. However, if you lodge in central Reykjavik, the nearby choice is the Sundholl Reykjavikur, the oldest public bath in Iceland, located just a few meters behind the Hallgrímskirkja church.

The pool is located in an old building that dates to 1937, and in 2007 the pool was renovated. Before, it only had one indoor pool and two outdoor hot tubs, but currently, it has one indoor and outdoor pool, two saunas, three hot tubes, one kid's pool, and a cold tub.

Another famous pool in the city is the Vesturbaejarlaug, located in the western area of the town. The pool is an outdoor one that has a few hot tubs and many saunas. It's one of the pools that Icelanders and visitors hang out in. And right across the street, near the pool, is a unique cafe, perfect for having a warm coffee or tea and dipping in the pool.

The largest pool in the city is the Laugardalslaug pool, located within the Reykjavik recreational center. This pool has a sports hall, botanical gardens, family park, zoo, sculpture museum, world-class gym, Laugar spa, and ice skating rink. So if you are with your family, Laugardalslaug is the best place for you to go all together.

Before entering the pools, you are required to get naked with the Icelanders. The action is not some ritual practice but for hygiene. The showers are based on gender, and because the pool has low chlorine levels, you must bathe thoroughly before entering the pool. Though this aside, most Reykjavik pools are open year-round so that you can enjoy them in all seasons.

●Visit the Hallgrímskirkja church

Around the city center is the famous Hallgrímskirkja church, which you can even view from every angle of Reykjavik. Among the places in the city, the church is the most well-known. And on top of the church, which is around 74.5 meters, is a viewing center to have a 360° view of the whole city. The tower is accessible every day except on Sundays since there is a service. Moreover, the church operates, so sometimes, it may be closed due to church activities happening inside. The entrance fee to the top is 7 USD for adults and 1 USD for kids aged 7-14 years; children younger than seven will have free entrance. The church was named after the pastor and poet Hallgrimur Pétursson. The basalt columns inspired the church's architecture at Svartifoss waterfall on Iceland's South Coast. Gudjon Samúelsson designed the building, and it was opened in 1986. The Church houses are Iceland's largest organs having 15 meters tall with 5,275 pipes and weighing 25 tons. Also, look at the entrance. It has a beautiful glass door designed by a local artist Leifur Breidfjord. When reaching the church, the first thing that will greet you is the statue of Leif Eriksson, who was one of the first Europeans to visit North America a thousand years before Columbus.

●**Explore by foot**

You can find many beautiful places in Reykjavik by simply walking on foot, which is the best advantage of this small town. From Hallgrímskirkja, explore the nearby streets on foot or take a bike if you don't want to walk. And to appreciate the culture more, it's best to visit the main shopping street, the Laugavegur, Bankastraeti, Austurstraeti, Laekjargata, and Skolavordustigur. You can access all these in the Reykjavik central area. Also, if you like shopping, you can visit the outdoor clothing chains selling extreme wear and outdoor gear. There are also plenty of small boutiques that sell good fashionable Icelandic designs. In addition, you will find many other places around Reykjavik that are worth a visit. For example, the Neighborhood of the Gods, the Thingholtin, and a lake in Reykjavik are located in the residential streets between Hallgrímskirkja church and Tjornin. The origin of most of the street names in this area is the Nordic language. For example, Odin's street is called Odinsgata, Thor's street- is Thorsgata, Loki's Path is Lokastigur, Freya's Street is Freyjugata, and many others. There are also plenty of colorful houses, fine gardens, and many street arts, and you are likely to bump into cats because, in Reykjavik, cats are common pets.

●**The Reykjavik city lake (Reykjavikurtjorn or just Tjornin)**

The city lake is one of the famous places tourists visit, especially those bird enthusiasts. You will find a bevy of swans and a raft of ducks in the place. The lake, at times, freezes in winter, which allows travelers to cross on foot, ice skate, or create a slippery football field. Near the lake is the Reykjavik City Hall, along with an extensive and informative Iceland 3D map. In addition, south of Nordic are the Nordic houses and Iceland's University.

The Nordic building is the only house designed by the international, famous Finnish-born architect Alvar Aalto. The Nordic homes often organize exhibitionists and live music, plus tasty restaurants. Going further, you will see the sea; from there, you can follow along Aegissida Street and watch the beautiful views of the North Atlantic. And from here, watching the sunset is pretty spectacular. East of the lake is the domestic airport and going further, you will see Nautholsvik Beach and the Oskjuhlid Hill forest. And from this site, you will find a beautiful city long from the top of the Perlan viewing center.

If you don't want to stay here, you can walk further west to the Grotta. In the area, you can find a lighthouse, beach, and Kvika, which is a scenic foot bath. Please remember that walking in the Grotta is long and laborious, so make it easy, rent a Hopp scooter, or reserve one day for your exploration. North of the lake is Austurvollur Square, a stunning way to have a get-together gathering with your family and friends. It's one of the famous spots if you want to host an event in Reykjavik in the summer. People visit the area to drink beer and sunbathe when the midnight sun appears. And during national celebrations, the city also hosts concerts and other public gatherings here. And when the citizens are upset about certain political activities, they come to this place to protest in the parliament around the square. On the side of the court are shops and cafes, and Domkirjhan, Reykjavik's oldest church, is behind the parliament.

●Visit the picturesque old harbor

You can visit the old harbor to learn about the history of marine life in Iceland and even read a book on whale watching trips.

●Visit the flea market, Kolaportid

If you stay in Reykjavik during the weekends, you can visit Kolaportid, the city's flea market. It's an eclectic market square where you can purchase things like a knitted wool sweater (Iceland's famous souvenir.) The market is situated at the Reykjavik harbor and contains multiple exciting items for sale, such as local delicacies like shellfish. The market atmosphere is lively and usually open from 11 am to 5 pm on weekends.

Walking a little more along the harbor, you'll find Reykjavik's fish-packing district, Grandi. Here, old fishing factories and boat repair shops are turned into shops, cafes, start-up companies, breweries, restaurants, and museums. One of the best examples of Reykjavik's changing face is Grandi. When you are here, go to Valdis to taste the best-known ice cream in the city or visit Bryggjan Brewery to drink one of the best locally made beers.

You can also visit the Marshall house, Iceland's museum of whales, or the Aurora Reykjavik Museum. Check out the beautiful street art on Vesturgata and appreciate the grassy hill, Thufa, and an outdoor art piece by Olof Nordal.

●Book local activities in the city

Reykjavik is a city filled with numerous surprises; in fact, on your own, you can discover many of its hidden gems and take advantage of them without even needing any guide. Furthermore, you can find many exciting activities to do near the city. If you don't like walking on foot, you can easily take a scenic helicopter ride over the city and appreciate all the sightseeing spots from the top; you can even view the tip of the surrounding mountain, Mt. Esjan. Other things you can do in the city, which are mostly available in most places in Iceland, include watching whales, birds, puffins, horse riding, etc. You can see whales like minke, whales, humpbacks, porpoises, and dolphins. You can also visit Videy, a famous island off the Reykjavik shore. Videy houses the Yoko Ono Imagine Peace Tower, which was erected in memory of John Lennon. Birds like gannets, gulls, cormorants, the Arctic tern, and puffins also frequently fly to the islands. So you will always find something to do in Reykjavik.

●Experience the nightlife in Reykjavik

Remember to add nightlife activities when listing things you will do in Reykjavik. Reykjavik's nightlife activities are generally famous among the locals. People party in the early hours, and when the bars and clubs are closed, the street remains filled with drunk people trying to find their way home or looking for after-party events. So whenever you are looking for something to do at night, you visit the bars and cafes that mainly offer live music concerts. The city always remains lively, with entertainment such as stand-up comedy, theatre, opera, jazz, drag shows, cabaret performance, and poetry brothels.

●Visit the Harpa Concert Hall

The Harpa Concert Hall is a big glass building close to the old harbor in Reykjavik. The iconic building architecture alone is impressive; you can admire it from both inside and outside and even snap some pictures.

●Try Iceland's local cuisine

In Reykjavik, you can eat some genuine and outstanding local cuisine. There are plenty of restaurants that specialize in serving local seafood and grilled meats. You can also find restaurants serving Thai, Italian, Mexican, Japanese, and even Ethiopian foods.

●Check out the Icelandic arts and culture

Aside from Harpa, which organizes a local live performance to watch art scenes, you can also visit museums, galleries, outdoor sculptures, and street art to appreciate the arts and cultures in Reykjavik.

Accommodations in Reykjavik

You can lodge in any of the following hotels.
●The Kex hostel Reykjavik at Skúlagata 28, 101 Reykjavik.
●Bus hostel at Skógarhlid 10, 105 Reykjavik
●Reykjavik peace center at 4522+C96, Vogasel, 109 Reykjavik.
●Reykjavik downtown hotel at Skolavordustigur 42, 101 Reykjavik
●4th-floor hotel at Laugavegur, 101 Reykjavik
●Fosshotel Reykjavik at þórunnartún 1, 105 Reykjavik
●Sand hotel by Keahotels at Laugavegur 34, 101 Reykjavik

Day 34: Vatnajokull Glacier

The Vatnajökull glacier is the largest in Europe, and it covers up to 8% of Iceland's landmass. The glacier is the most attractive feature of the Vatnajökull National Park; the park is a popular hiking area, boat tours, ice caving tours, etc. The Vatnajökull National Park was established in 2008.

How to reach the Vatnajökull National Park
From Reykjavik, you can easily access the park.

The Vatnajökull in culture
Many films were shot in Vatnajökull. The first film scene was James Bond's A View to Kill in 1985, followed by some notable scenes in Batman Begins, Lara Croft, Tomb Raider, and Game of Thrones.

Day 35: Lofthellir ice cave

The lofthellir ice cave is a cave inside a Lava tunnel containing ice formations from hundreds of years ago. We can say this place is a lost world of ice and magic, frozen in time and place. The cave is well-protected and owned by local landowners. Only a few people are allowed to the site, and the Geo Travel Certified Cave Guides operate it. The goal of preserving the cave is maintaining it and keeping it for future generations to explore.

So if you are able to buy the tickets, you will find that the fee includes money for protection programs and the local landowners. Once you reach the cave, you will be provided a helmet, headlamp, and studded boots before entering the ice cave. You will walk into the cave slowly in a single line with the help of your guide. The entrance is narrow, but the cave gets wider with every step you take.

Day 36: Eyjafjordur

Up north, Iceland is a beautiful fjord called the Eyjafjördur fjord. It's about sixty kilometers long from the beginning to the end and is the longest fjord in North Iceland. The site is home to many exciting places that are worth visiting.

Eyjafjördur is at the Arctic Circle edge and has two beautiful islands, Hrísey island, and Grimsey Island. We have already discussed Grimsey Island, so we will only describe Hrísey Island, which is the Pearl of Eyjafjördur.

●Sail to Hrísey

Hrísey is the country's second biggest island, with 180 to 190 residents. 7.5 kilometers long and 2.5 kilometers wide. Once you arrive at the Island, the first the that will greet you is a taxi on the island. You will see a tractor with a hay cat that can transport a few people. The cab will be your guide and take you on a 40-minute trip around the island. Alternatively, the island is not that big so that you can walk around on foot.

On your tour, you will see convenience stores, a church, restaurants and guesthouses, a campsite, and a swimming pool. The village's oldest house is the red Hús Hákarla Jörundar. Or call the house of Shark Jörundur. It was built in 1886 and is now a museum that tells the history of Iceland's shark fishing for centuries.

The village's primary industry is a small fishing vessel fishery, blue Mussel breeding, and summer tourism. The village's herring industry was booming in the mid-20th century and is the second largest Herring port in North Iceland after Siglufjordur. But now, the herring business has disappeared, and things have already changed. Order a beefsteak in Restaurant Brekka from the Galloway breed.

You can visit the Hríseyjarkirkja church, snap some photos and keep memories. Hrísey is a peaceful village where you will find homes used as summer houses. Aside from that, the town is a bird-watching paradise; you can find more than 40 species of birds nesting on the island, and even Ptarmigan is in abundance here.

●**The ferry sævar**
   If you are following the ferry sævar, then note that it leaves nine times a day from Ársskógssandur and only takes fifteen minutes to drive to the Island. So buy the ticket at the accommodation ladder while entering the ferry.

●**Angelica**
   In Hrísey, you will find Angelica (Hvönn) in abundance, which is used for health products of saga medical. And from Hrísey, just opposite the sea, is a brewing factory that serves good beer, and the beer is called Kaldi. Here, from the restaurants, you can even bathe in a young beer in wooden kegs. You can also sit outside in barrels inside Geothermal water.

●The Porgeirsboli Ghost

Your visit to Hrísey is incomplete if you didn't visit the site of the most horrific ghost in Iceland (that's if you are fond of scary activities.) Folklore said in the 18th century, porgeirsboli was filled with ghosts, according to Galera Geiri, who conjured up the horrible ghost. Icelanders living in Hrísey could sense the ghost's presence. A woman rejected Galdra's love, so he conjured a spirit to haunt the woman. The ghost grew stronger by the day and hunted Galdra and his family. Some even said the ghost is currently out somewhere roaming around.

Day 37: Hringsbjarg Cliff on Tjörness peninsula

On the East Tjörness peninsula is a 60 meters tall cliff. From the ridge, you can have a stunning view of Fjallahôfn and a massive view of Kelduhverfi county. This cliff is an excellent place to view during puffin season. You will watch the beautiful beak and orange feet bird that will keep you in awe.

You will find an observation platform on the cliff to watch the fantastic view. Moreover, the platform is for safety. Once you reach the cliff area, you will see a parking space above the observation platform and an information sign.

How to reach the cliff

The best way to reach the platform is to drive from Húsavík, close to the site. The best time to have a fantastic view is to visit the cliff on sunny days, don't forget to carry binoculars to have excellent bird watching. In addition, you can see lagoons and rivers from the lakes, one of the lakes is even the Skjálftavatn or Lake Earthquake. From the cliff, you can also view the

Melkrakkaslétta plain.

The driftwood beach

From Hringsbjarg, following road 85 is a beach filled with driftwood. Parking and walking on the beach are a lot of fun. Driftwood has been a valuable asset to Icelanders for centuries. The people there use driftwood to make furniture and construction instead of coals; the sea salt makes the wood hard and suitable for this kind of work. The north Iceland driftwood comes from Siberia.

Check the View-Dial at Imbubúfa in Kelduhverfi

In Kelduhverfi, you will see another lovely spot with a fantastic view of the vast area. This place is called Imbubúfa. On the hill's top, which is around 132 meters above sea level, is a view dial made by Jakob Hálfdanarson in 1980. The view dial contains the names and heights of the mountains in the area. Iceland's president at that time, Vigdís Finnbogadóttir, was the first person invited to see the view dial.

A tale of Imbubúfa says that the place is haunted. Some strange-sounding names from a ghost believed to be haunting the place. The ghost's name is imba, and he was said to be traveling in the area during a snowstorm and doesn't know he has come to the cliff's edge, fell, and died. After her tragic death, Imba is believed to have been haunting the area. To reach the top of the Imbubúfa, follow gravel from road 85 opposite the Hringsbjarg. Follow the Kelduhverfi and hringsjá signs.

Day 38: Gjastykki

Gjádtykki is an extraordinary and colorful lava field where you can see newly formed lava formations from Krafla volcanic eruptions.

How to reach Gjádtykki

To reach Gjástykki, drive throughout the Krafla area on a paved road and turn into a bumpy road after a while. (If you tend to get carsick quickly, ask the driver to allow you to sit in the front because the road is not in good condition.) On the way, you will see a tire that leads up to a steep hill; drive up the steep hill.

Once you reach the top, you will be greeted with a unique view of the Krafla area. Stop by another hill called the Hreindyrahóll, which is 3 km away from Viti, and appreciate the beautiful view of the area.

When you reach the Gjásttykki main area, you can see from above the directions of the black lava flow and where it stops. You can evidently see the difference between the black lava and the green grass.

●Hike the Gjásttykki

Once you appreciate those areas, it's time to start your 1.5-hour bike in the Gjásttykki rift valley. You will surely be amazed by the black lava stretch and be excited to see this place. While hiking, you will first encounter something that resembles a dinosaur egg filled with colorful lava. When you look around, you will see piles of lava with an opening top. They are lava formations with gas trapped in them; you can even feel the heat from the holes.

They are bubbles so visible that you can vividly see what's inside them. You will see a colorful opening at the top of the bubble, emitting heat. In Gjástykki, there are plenty of lava formations called slag. People often visit the place because most of the lava is newly formed, so they are sensitive and brittle. In addition, geologists have a field here in Gjásttykki to examine new lava formations and how they affect the landscape.

Day 39: Pingvellir National Park

The Pingvellir National Park is one of the sorted tourist attractions in North Iceland, mainly because of its history and geology. In the national park, you can watch the geological process playing out. It's where the nation's history began, and most of its major historical turns were created. Simply, it's a place filled with wealth and many things to do.

From February 2015 to February 2016, more than seven hundred thousand people visited the park, making it among the most visited sites in the country. From Reykjavik, it will take only 45 minutes to reach the park. Today, people visit this place not only for its History and geology but also to enjoy snorkeling and diving.

The tectonic environment opens the ravines, filled with the meltwater from the Longjökull glacier. It traveled underground for so many years through the lava rock and underwent thorough filtration. So it's clean and crystal clear in the ravines. Silfra is the most famous ravine and the only accessible one to go snorkeling or diving in. You can see the water vividly for more than 100 meters, allowing you to dip yourself in the magical blue world and experience the fantastic geology beneath it. Silfra is considered one of the world's top dive sites because of its uniqueness. To participate in the scuba dive, you are required to have a drysuit certificate or at least ten logged dives in a drysuit or verified by a professional guide. The requirements are few, but you must at least be 12 years old and can swim.

●Game of Thrones shooting location.

Another reason people visit Pingvellir is to see the popular HBO series Game of Thrones locations. You can even snap one or two shots here. The Almannagjá mentioned above was used as the Moon Gates, home of Lady Lysa, Jon Arryn's widow.

●Wildlife

Another thing that drags people to Pingvellir is animal life. You can fish in the lake and watch birds in the summer. In addition, if you are a wildlife enthusiast, you can keep your eye on the undergrowth and the water edges for Arctic Foxes and Mink.

Although visiting Pingvellir is rewarding and will give you a good experience, the area's infrastructure is declining because of the negative effect of nature. A delicate moss has covered most of the part, and people who have not stuck to the paths damaged it during their visit, which may likely take years to recover. The 'wishing well' heavy metals people have thrown into the lakes are now visible above. And some people that stayed at the campsite left their waste. All these are a few of the ways visitors have damaged the park.

So as a visitor, you should respect the park's survival by following the basic rules and leaving as small an impact as possible to maintain the place's hygiene. Ideally, the park is a place that will keep you wanting to visit again because of its beauty and culture.

Day 40: Skutustadir Pseudo Craters

The pseudo craters can be found in most places worldwide, and Iceland is among them. Already, Iceland is a feast; now, the Pseudo Craters are just another unique addition to that feast. Skutustadir PseudoCraters are the most prominent craters in Iceland, located in the Myvatn area. The craters are part of plenty of extraordinary sights in the Myvatn area and are among the most fascinating natural phenomena in the country.

The hot lava created the craters to boil the wetlands' water, and the steam pressure led to the explosions, thus forming the pseudo-crater clusters.

The craters were formed 2,300 years ago during the Lú-dentaborgir and prengslaborgir eruptions. On the scoria mount sits the clusters of the craters, adding uniqueness. The Skútustadagigar is the most spectacular Crater in Iceland because of its distinctive looks that resemble big bowls. The place is easy to visit since it's just by the road.

And from there, you can follow a path that takes you on an

exciting walk in the beautiful rootless craters, and you can even see Lake Myvatn.

Pseudo craters are sometimes called rootless or rootless cones because they don't have an end and aren't connected to the magma conduit. If plenty of eruptions happen, they resemble normal volcanic craters, and you might even think they are actual craters that erupt. If the explosion didn't happen, the place might look like hills, not Volcanic bowls.

When you visit the craters, indeed the difference between them. Some are grassy hills; others have volcanic bowls, while others have other variations, such as lava cones with lava spatter and scoria. In 1973, skútustadagigar was protected as a natural monument.

Chapter 6

North Iceland's VAT refund info

If you visit Iceland and are about to leave, you can buy goods and services free of VAT.

So what's this VAT?

Value Added Tax is a multi-stage sales tax levied on the price of things you purchase. VAT is a consumption tax paid when you buy goods and services. So, whenever you purchase something, keep the receipt so the purchase can be verified for reimbursement.

VAT refunds rules in Iceland

You can get your VAT refund if you aren't staying in Iceland when you purchase goods and services as far as you have to abide by the Conditions of Regulations No. 1188/2014. To get a refund, you must be a non-Iceland resident. You will provide your passport or ID card that clearly verifies that you are a resident of another country, not Iceland. You are not entitled to a VAT refund if you are a foreigner permanently living in the country.

The following conditions must be met if you want to be eligible for VAT refunds.

1. You must bring the goods out of the country within three months of your purchase.
2. The price of the items, including VAT, must be at least 6,000ISK
3. When leaving, you must present the goods and the requisite documentation.

Where to get your VAT refunds

You can get your VAT refund at Arion Bank, located at the arrival hall opposite the car rentals. You must reclaim your VAT before checking in your luggage.

I truly hope this book is a blessing to you and help feel adventurous enough to explore more of this world God created. Could you do me a favor? Please leave an honest review on Amazon. Reviews mean the world to an author. You can also connect with me on Facebook, Twitter, or Instagram for upcoming releases or to chat. I look forward to it!

https://www.alexrollins.website

https://www.facebook.com/people/Alex-Rollins/100086978462112/

Conclusion

Iceland generally is defined by its landscape, volcanoes, geysers, hot springs, and lava fields. The country is filled with activities for both locals and tourists. Whenever you are planning a trip to Iceland, then go North. North Iceland is worth visiting; it is vibrant, unique, and filled with fascinating and attractive wildlife. In North Iceland, you can find multiple destinations for tourists like you; the locals there are welcoming, and in many places, you don't even have to worry about your money as the entrance there is free. In North Iceland, places like the Arctic henge, a giant stone sculpture in the northwestern ball he Raufarhöfn, will give you joy. Not to talk of the Askja area has three geothermal lakes, the Askja lake, Öskjuvatn Lake, and the Viti volcano lake. You can watch different wildlife such as birds, whales and a lot more. You can also soak in a beer spa in Dalvik, feel the magic of the Myvatn Area, and voyage to Grimsey Island and many other places. All in all, North Iceland is a must-visit place. So next time you plan a vacation, visit North Iceland; you will never feel bored there.

Resources

1. https://www.britannica.com/place/Iceland#:~:text=Ice
   land%20was%20founded%20more%20than,which%20th
   e%20Norse%20called%20Vinland
2. https://weather-and-climate.com/average-monthly-Rai
   nfall-Temperature-Sunshine-region-north-iceland-is,Ic
   eland
3. https://www.mountainguides.is/northern-lights-icelan
   d?gclid=CjwKCAjw4c-ZBhAEEiwAZ105RcZt9JLnEO
   OntQLcDP3SjBafe5vFUrXxJ95kR_GkLT82rujgHOIYi
   xoCizwQAvD_BwE
4. https://iceland.nordicvisitor.com/travel-guide/informa
   tion/what-to-pack/
5. https://fullsuitcase.com/siglufjordur-iceland/
6. https://guidetoiceland.is/connect-with-locals/regina/gr
   imsey-island-express-the-gem-of-the-arctic-circle
7. https://www.northsailing.is/2018/01/07/top-5-things-
   to-do-in-husavik/
8. https://guidetoiceland.is/connect-with-locals/aldasigm
   unds/three-great-reasons-for-visiting-beautiful-hofsos-
   besides-the-fact-that-its-beautiful
9. https://guidetoiceland.is/travel-iceland/drive/dalvik

10. https://www.laidbacktrip.com/posts/asbyrgi-canyon-guide
11. https://adventures.com/iceland/attractions/lakes-lagoons/lake-myvatn/
12. https://guidetoiceland.is/best-of-iceland/top-things-to-do-in-akureyri
13. https://www.zigzagonearth.com/grjotagja-cave-iceland/
14. https://www.funiceland.is/nature/natural-pools/grettislaug/
15. https://www.northiceland.is/en/service/the-transportation-museum-at-ystafell
16. https://guidetoiceland.is/connect-with-travel-bloggers/639/how-to-visit-askja-in-the-highlands
17. https://www.vatnajokulsthjodgardur.is/en/areas/jokulsargljufur
18. https://www.zigzagonearth.com/hverir-myvatn-iceland/
19. https://guidetoiceland.is/connect-with-locals/regina/hvitserkur-up-north
20. https://www.northiceland.is/en/place/arctic-henge
21. https://guidetoiceland.is/connect-with-locals/regina/drangey-bird-cliff-in-north-iceland
22. https://www.laidbacktrip.com/posts/kolugljufur-canyon-kolufoss-waterfall-iceland
23. https://www.icelandtravel.is/attractions/reykjavik-2-2/
24. https://guidetoiceland.is/connect-with-locals/regina/eyjafjorur-fjord-in-north-iceland-part-i
25. https://guidetoiceland.is/travel-iceland/drive/gjastykki
26. https://guidetoiceland.is/connect-with-locals/jorunnsg

/ingvellir-national-park
27. https://www.guide.is/places/detail/skutustadir-pseudo
craters-myvatn-north-iceland

www.ingramcontent.com/pod-product-compliance
Lightning Source LLC
Chambersburg PA
CBHW031410150726
47989CB00002B/594